"When you've got all fi
your legs work, it's easy to miss how often
society neglects those for whom this isn't true.
In **Everyone's Universe**, Noreen Grice,
a uniquely inspired champion of astronomy
education, has identified activities and places in
America where, no matter your level of sensory
or physical limitation, the universe is accessible
to all. As it should be."

— Neil deGrasse Tyson
Astrophysicist & Director, Hayden Planetarium
American Museum of Natural History

"I am convinced that by incorporating Noreen's
unique brand of accessibility into our star
parties, talks, and other astronomy programs,
we will make our activities more relevant
for society at large.... We may create little
miracles of perception and open windows to
infinity.... And we will reap great rewards of
satisfaction and enjoyment!"

—Steve Dodson, Stargazer Steve

"In a practical and powerful way **Everyone's Universe** establishes the twenty-first century paradigm for engaging everyone in the wonder of astronomical exploration. The experience, innovation, and passion that Noreen Grice brings together in this new resource is certain to help create a new movement of backyard astronomers."

— Mark Riccobono, Executive Director
Jernigan Institute
National Federation of the Blind

"**Everyone's Universe** will be invaluable to those facing an accessibility issue, allowing everyone to enjoy the beauty of the sky."

—David Eicher, Astronomy Magazine

"This is one helpful volume on a subject for which I received no training when I was new to the planetarium profession."

—April Whitt, International Planetarium Society

"Most of the universe may be out of reach, but it's not inaccessible. Noreen Grice is determined to make it more accessible. She has pioneered accessible astronomy for nearly three decades and has developed innovations that download the sky into the hands of those whose grasp it eluded. Her new book is a marvel of encouragement and practical advice. It will certainly expand the universe of accessible astronomy. **Everyone's Universe** shows how it's already being done and how easy it is to get everyone in touch with the sky."

—Dr. E.C. Krupp, Director
Griffith Observatory
Los Angeles

"**Everyone's Universe** is a must-read for anyone involved in astronomy outreach and should be in possession of every astronomy club and facility that deals with the general public."

—Glenn Chaple, Astronomy Magazine

"Noreen Grice has done a great job creating a must-have guide on how to make the universe more accessible."

—Damien Wimbush
Assistive Technology Training Programs Manager
California State University Northridge
Center on Disabilities

Everyone's Universe

OTHER BOOKS BY NOREEN GRICE

Touch the Stars

Touch the Universe
  A NASA Braille Book of Astronomy

Touch the Sun
  A NASA Braille Book

The Little Moon Phase Book

Touch the Invisible Sky
  A Multi-Wavelength Braille Book
  Featuring Tactile NASA Images

Everyone's Universe

SECOND EDITION

A Guide to Accessible Astronomy Places

by Noreen Grice

You Can Do Astronomy • New Britain, Connecticut

Everyone's Universe
A Guide to Accessible Astronomy Places
By Noreen Grice

Second Edition

Published by
You Can Do Astronomy LLC
New Britain, Connecticut

Visit us at www.youcandoastronomy.com

© 2011–2012 Noreen Grice. All rights reserved.

ISBN: 978-0-9833567-3-8
Library of Congress Control Number: 2012939068

Manufactured in the United States of America

Large Print | This book is designed to the large print standard. The body text is 16/22 Gill Sans.

Design and composition: www.dmargulis.com

Symbols Used in This Book

 Wheelchair accessible facility or portable telescopes available

 Braille or tactile materials available

 Accessibility for low vision (telescopic image visible on monitor)

 Accessibility for individuals with neurological disorders

 Augmentative and alternative communication

 Captioning available

 Assistive listening devices available

 Sign language available (but may require advance notice)

About the Author

Lorraine Greenfield

Noreen Grice holds a bachelor's degree in astronomy from Boston University, a master's degree in astronomy from San Diego State University, and professional certificates in museum studies (Tufts University), nonprofit management (Boston Center for Adult Education), and assistive technology applications (California State University, Northridge).

She worked in the planetarium field for 26 years and found creative ways to make astronomy education more accessible to people with disabilities. Noreen is the author of several books, including **Touch the Stars** (National Braille Press); **Touch the Universe: A NASA Braille Book of Astronomy** and **Touch the Sun: A NASA Braille Book** (Joseph Henry Press); and **The Little Moon Phase Book** and **Touch the Invisible Sky: A Multi-Wavelength Braille Book Featuring Tactile NASA Images** (Ozone Publishing).

Noreen is the recipient of many awards, including the Klumpke-Roberts Award (Astronomical Society of the Pacific) and the Jacob Bolotin Award (National Federation of the Blind). She is founder and president of You Can Do Astronomy LLC. Her mission is to make astronomy education accessible for everyone, regardless of (dis)ability, and she never accepts that something is impossible!

You can read more about her work at www.youcandoastronomy.com.

Contents

Part I: How to Make the Universe Accessible   I

Preface

In 1984, a group of students who were blind came to my planetarium show. At the end of the program I asked them how they liked it. They told me exactly how they felt. "It stunk," they said as they walked down the hallway.

That was a jolt for me because I never considered that astronomy was not accessible until this group of students pointed that out to me. I felt terrible. I was embarrassed that I had been so unprepared. I thought the planetarium was the most wonderful place in the world. Clearly, for this group, it was not.

This experience was profound for me. I decided to develop strategies and resources to make astronomy accessible for everyone, regardless of their (dis)ability. Rather than focusing on limitations, I began creating resources and models that could be used by a broad range of people of different abilities and learning styles. I knew that my success would come from educational materials and strategies that would bring people together. The more time people spent together, the more barriers of difference would disappear until people just saw each other as people, with a disability not being the first thing they noticed.

Acknowledgments

When I began writing the first edition of **Everyone's Universe**, I envisioned a unique resource guide for both astronomy educators and space science enthusiasts. This book would fill a gap in making astronomy more accessible and help bring the night sky to the fingertips of new participants.

Everyone's Universe would not have been possible without the help of many people. Thank you to the individuals and organizations, listed in this guide, who responded to my inquiries and wanted to share their accessibility options with others. Thank you to my wonderful husband, Dennis, and my mother, Edith, for their continued support and belief in my work, and to my national and international colleagues in science museums, astronomy clubs, observatories, and planetariums. Additional thanks to Dr. Ernest Panscofar (Central Connecticut State University), who provided thoughtful comments about topics in special education, to Ms. Mary Winchell (American School for the Deaf) for her suggestions on making museum tours more accessible for hearing-impaired visitors, and to Ms. Rachel McGeehan (Matthew's mom) for sharing her museum experiences as the mother of a child with autism.

This second, expanded edition would not have been possible without Dick Margulis, who has served as my editor and book designer for both editions of **Everyone's Universe**. Marilyn Augst created the index for the second edition.

I hope you will use and enjoy this book and visit many of the wonderful facilities featured inside. Accessible astronomy comes in many forms and is offered in many places, and we all benefit.

Please join in! We can make the universe more accessible together!

Introduction

Disability and Accessibility

As you are reading these words, someone, somewhere in the world, is looking through a telescope for the first time, getting a closer view of the night sky. Maybe this person is looking at the heavens from their backyard telescope or through a telescope staffed by an amateur astronomer.

If you're interested in helping people with disabilities share your passion for astronomy, read the next section, "For the Astronomy Educator." If you yourself are a person with a disability or an advocate or family member of a person with a disability, read the section headed "For the Astronomy Participant."

For the Astronomy Educator

Astronomy club members often set up telescopes in places like museums, schools, parks, and beaches, inviting the local community to peer at distant objects through the eyepiece of a telescope. These gatherings are called star parties, and the excitement of participants is contagious.

Each state is home to astronomy clubs, planetariums, and observatories. The organizers of star parties plan for a crowd of excited students, families, and adults. They know that a person's first peek at the Moon, Jupiter's red spot, or Saturn's rings will amaze them and inspire them to look up at the night sky on their own.

Now imagine this. You are standing at your telescope waiting for the next interested person to take a peek, when you notice someone in a wheelchair approaching you. All you can think of is "what should I do?"

Let's begin with a few facts. The Americans with Disabilities Act defines a person with a disability as:

A. having a physical or mental impairment that substantially limits one or more of the major life activities of such an individual;
B. having a record of such an impairment; or
C. being regarded as having such impairment.

According to the U.S. Department of Commerce's 1997 Census Brief, about one in every five Americans has some kind of disability. That's a lot of people, and this statistic is expected to increase as the population ages.

Now combine the people who have some kind of disability with the people they like to socialize with—their family and friends—and you begin to understand the increased possibility that you will encounter a person with a disability at one of your science programs. There's nothing wrong with this scene unless you are not prepared to welcome a variety of visitors. That's where this guide can help.

The first section of this book is written for the astronomy educator. Here, you will read about strategies for making an educational event accessible and welcoming for people of all abilities.

For the Astronomy Participant

If you are the person with a disability, how do you know whether your local observatory, science museum, or planetarium is accessible? This information is not always easily located on a website. What can you do as an individual to improve access for yourself and others?

The second part of this book is a resource directory for a person looking to visit an already accessible astronomy place, such as an observatory or planetarium. Yes, there are accessible places, and this guide will tell you where they are!

Consider donating a copy of this book to your local astronomy club, observatory, or planetarium so they can be more accessible, too!

Everyone's Universe

Part I

How to Make the Universe Accessible

Chapter 1

Mobility-Friendly Observing

Visualize the following three scenarios.

- A group of astronomy enthusiasts gathers on a hill with their telescopes and invites others to share their view of the night sky.
- A museum opens its rooftop observatory once a week. Visitors walk up the spiral staircase to the observatory platform. There they are treated to a view through the telescope.
- University students staff telescopes for public open nights. Visitors listen to a lecture and, weather permitting, may climb the ladder chair to peer through a historic refractor telescope.

These three scenarios describe opportunities to view celestial objects through a telescope. Maybe you were inspired to learn more about astronomy by attending observing sessions like these. But people who travel in a wheelchair, have difficulty walking, or have other challenges often encounter unnecessary barriers.

It is **not** all right to say "This is how we have always done it" or "We are exempt" and dismiss a population of people from experiencing the excitement of viewing the night sky through a telescope. Informal science programs can be made accessible and inviting to a broader range of participants by planning proactively with the participant in mind.

Many older observatories were designed for people to walk up spiral staircases to reach the telescope chamber. The observer then may also need to climb a ladder to view objects through the eyepiece. This might be the traditional observatory setup, but it is inaccessible to people who cannot walk or climb stairs.

Telescopes can be designed to be accessible to people viewing from a seated position. Many of the newer observatories are designed to be accessible to a broader range of participants. Let's take a closer look at some of them.

SPOTLIGHT
Wren-Marcario Accessible Telescope
McDonald Observatory, Mt. Locke, Texas

The University of Texas at Austin's McDonald Observatory unveiled an accessible telescope for wheelchair users in the summer of 2010. Guests follow a wheelchair accessible path from the Visitor Center to a plaza with a unique optical instrument. The Wren-Marcario Accessible Telescope (WMAT) consists of two 18-inch (46 cm) primary mirrors aligned north and south. A flat steering mirror between the primary mirrors allows the user to easily move between sky objects, as the eyepiece remains fixed. The WMAT is staffed by a telescope operator and is available for everyone to use.

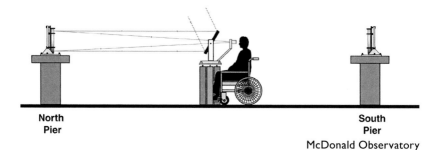

North Pier   **South Pier**

McDonald Observatory

Wren-Marcario Accessible Telescope

McDonald Observatory

A visitor using the Wren-Marcario Accessible Telescope (WMAT) at the McDonald Observatory. A staff person from McDonald Observatory looks on.

SPOTLIGHT
J. J. McCarthy Observatory
New Milford, Connecticut

The McCarthy Observatory is located in New Milford, Connecticut, on the grounds of New Milford High School. The facility is used for both education and research. It is available for students, local community groups, teachers, scientists, and the general public at no charge. Donors and charitable grants pay operating costs.

The McCarthy Observatory opened in 2000 as a wheelchair-friendly facility. Visitors enter the observatory building from street level, and a wheelchair lift transports people to the observing platform of the 16-inch (40 cm) telescope.

How do you make the eyepiece accessible when the telescope is focused on low sky objects? Staff from the McCarthy Observatory designed a flexible, coherent bundle of fiber-optic strands enclosed in a braided metallic sheath, as an eyepiece extender. The custom-made eyepiece extender, built by Schott Optical, mounts on a standard 1¼-inch (32 mm) eyepiece and brings the image about three feet (1 m) to observers in a seated position, who can then focus the image themselves. This allows a visitor with a mobility limitation the opportunity to actively participate in viewing sessions.

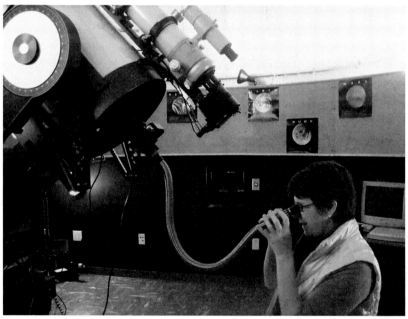

Monty Robson, McCarthy Observatory

Eyepiece extender in use at McCarthy Observatory

SPOTLIGHT
ARE-125 Eyepiece
DFM Engineering

Observatories that want to purchase an extended eyepiece for their large telescope may be interested in a product called the ARE-125. DFM Engineering Inc. in Longmont, Colorado, was founded by Frank Melsheimer, an authority on telescope design and manufacture. Dr. Melsheimer wanted to make telescopes more accessible to people who could not stand or walk.

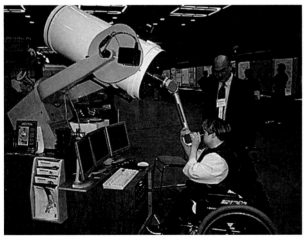

DFM Engineering

Frank Melsheimer with patron, demonstrating the ARE-125 eyepiece

He created the articulated relay eyepiece (ARE). Originally designed to work with DFM telescopes, the ARE-125 can be used to work with any *f*/8 or slower telescope fitted with a standard 2-inch (5 cm) focuser.

The ARE-125 is an extension arm that connects to the telescope and uses a series of mirrors and relay lenses mounted within the arm to reposition the image down to the eyepiece. An observer in a seated position is able to move the arm in three axes to comfortably see through the telescope.

SPOTLIGHT
Centennial Observatory
College of Southern Idaho, Twin Falls

The Centennial Observatory is located on the campus of the College of Southern Idaho and is one of the astronomy facilities that use the ARE-125 eyepiece extender. A wheelchair lift brings visitors from the observatory lobby to the floor level of the observatory dome, where the extended eyepiece is available for use.

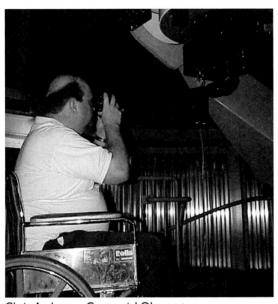

Chris Andersen, Centennial Observatory

ARE-125 eyepiece extender in use at Centennial Observatory

Observing from Ground Level

Does your observatory require visitors to walk up stairs to the observing platform? Is it physically impossible for a person in a wheelchair or electric scooter to gain access to the observing platform because you simply have no room to add in a wheelchair ramp or lift? One way to provide accessibility to an older observatory is to attach a video camera to the telescope eyepiece and transmit the image to a monitor at ground level. A large image from the telescope then would be accessible to anyone, regardless of physical limitations. This setup is also great for parents who may prefer not to climb a staircase when they are using baby strollers or accompanying young children.

SPOTLIGHT
Santa Barbara Astronomical Unit
Santa Barbara, California

The Santa Barbara Astronomical Unit (SBAU) is an organization of more than a hundred members. Weather permitting, SBAU offers monthly star parties at the Santa Barbara Museum of Natural History, at nearby Westmonth College, and at Camino Real Marketplace. In addition, summer star parties are held at campgrounds and state beaches. But that's not all. During the year, SBAU brings telescopes and astronomy programs to local schools, hotels, elderhostels, wineries, scout events, corporate events, and the annual Avocado Festival in Carpinteria. All together, they staff about 200 outreach events every year.

In 2011, SBAU received the Out-of-This-World Award from Astronomy magazine for their efforts in bringing 16,000 people access to telescopes and amateur astronomy help the previous year. They used the funds from this award to pay for manufacture of a wheelchair accessible telescope mount, called the UC2 ("you see too"). Designed by SBAU member Jim Williams, the UC2 mount allows people seated in wheelchairs easy access to the telescope eyepiece. A motorcycle jack is used to raise and lower the mount, and a large cantilever arm provides clearance under the telescope for wheelchairs.

The UC2 mount is used for public outreach at the Santa Barbara Museum of Natural History and beyond the museum. A unique sign depicting a person in a wheelchair viewing with a telescope identifies the UC2 accessible viewing area.

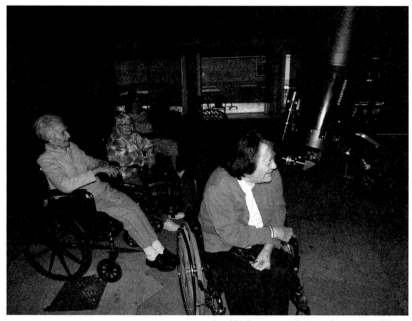

Jim Williams and Ruben Gutierrez, SBAU

Nursing home resident viewing through telescope eyepiece with telescope attached to the UC2 mount

Jim Williams, SBAU

The special sign identifying the accessible viewing area

SPOTLIGHT
FAR Laboratories
South Hadley, Massachusetts

Alan Rifkin is an amateur astronomer who designs telescope mounts and observing systems. His company is called FAR Laboratories, and his motto is "All You Add Is the Sky."

FAR Laboratories supports equal access for telescope viewing. It developed and sells the Dyna Pier Angled Mount. A telescope is attached to the end of the Dyna Pier arm, providing access for a person in a wheelchair to view from the eyepiece. The mount and floor plate can be set up by one person in a few minutes, creating an accessible viewing area.

The Dyna Pier Angled Mount can support a telescope that is no larger than an 8-inch Schmidt-Cassegrain (SCT). Alan takes this special mount to outreach events with the

Springfield (Massachusetts) STARS (astronomy) club, including their "Music Under the Stars" program at Tanglewood.

FAR Laboratories also designs a railing system where multiple telescopes can be mounted. For more information on FAR Laboratories "Handicapped Access to the Sky" designs, go to http://www.dynapod. com/dyna-hp.html.

FAR Laboratores

Dyna Pier Angled Mount

Another way to provide accessibility is to have a portable telescope available at ground level, along with an experienced guide to the night sky.

A compact, lightweight, and portable telescope, such as an Edmund Scientific Astroscan Telescope or a Celestron FirstScope, placed on a low table, allows a person in a wheelchair to physically move the telescope and independently observe the night sky.

A Dobsonian telescope can also allow the participant to view highlighted objects and

Edmund Scientific
Astroscan Telescope

Celestron Telescopes
Celestron FirstScope
Telescope

independently explore the night sky. Dobsonian telescopes are convenient to use because they are low to the ground. However, some people (especially young kids) tend to grab the eyepiece without realizing that they are moving the telescope out of alignment with the object. As with any telescope, it is recommended that an astronomy guide be present to assist with and monitor use of the telescope and provide assistance in aligning the telescope to a sky object.

Orion Dobsonian Telescope
Reprinted with permission from Orion Telescopes & Binoculars

If the Dobsonian telescope has an aperture of six to eight inches (15 to 20 cm), the tube should be short enough for a person in a wheelchair to maneuver in order to view through the eyepiece.

In summary, for a star party to be accessible for a variety of participants, it is best to avoid stairs, ladders, and uneven surfaces. Telescopes that are accessible by elevator or at ground level, and images transmitted remotely from the telescope, allow access for people with mobility challenges.

Chapter 2

Visual-Friendly Observing

There are several strategies for making observing more accessible to people with visual impairment.

Touchable Telescopes

Provide a tactile guided tour of the observing equipment. Vividly explain how the telescope works. With permission, guide the person's hand along accessible parts of the telescope. For small telescopes, this is easy, as the equipment will be at arm's length. For large telescopes and telescopes in observatories, be creative. Have a ruler or a yard- or meter stick handy and hold it up to the telescope, carefully guiding the person's reach along the side of the telescope. Describe how long and wide the telescope is.

Andy Cheng, Texas Astronomical Society of Dallas

Tactile tour of a telescope

Explain how the light enters the telescope and makes its way to the eyepiece. Describe the environment around the telescope. If you are in a dome, move the dome so the person can hear and feel the dome motor; but warn the person first, especially if they have a service animal that might be startled.

You might also consider creating a hands-on model of a telescope by cutting a non-useable telescope in half lengthwise or building a simple model and gluing the lenses and mirrors permanently in place. This hands-on model will help you explain the path of light through a telescope and the optical components inside. No doubt you will also find that people without visual impairment benefit from this accessible model.

Tactile Image Library

The people who attend your astronomy program come because they are interested in learning about space science. This includes children, adults, and people of all ages who have different learning styles. You probably already have a few star maps handy to show people constellations, but consider creating an accessible resource collection that is available at all times.

For example, **Touch the Stars** is an astronomy book with Braille and print text. The images are raised line drawings on plastic pages, with accompanying Braille labels. The tactile illustrations include star patterns, planets, moon phases, eclipses, nebulae, and galaxies.

The Thinktank Science Center in Birmingham, England, has a copy of **Touch the Stars** that they have annotated for quick reference. Their live planetarium shows are designed to present topics in the same order that they appear in **Touch the Stars**. They are prepared to provide, without hesitation, tactile images for any person who needs them.

Mario DiMaggio, Thinktank Planetarium

A well-used copy of **Touch the Stars** at the Thinktank Science Center

You can also create your own tactile models from supplies at a local arts and crafts store. Make planets out of Styrofoam balls or galaxies out of foam paper. The possibilities are endless.

The author, at age 14, stands behind a table with tactile models used for a science fair project.

Tactile images are also useful for sighted students as a preview of what they will be viewing through the telescope. If you have a tactile image of the object in the telescope, you can invite people to examine it while they are waiting in line for the telescope. Jim Stryder, a NASA educator, provides tactile pictures for visitors to use at his outreach programs.

Jim Stryder

Students touch a tactile image of Saturn in **Touch the Universe** before they look through the telescope.

Jim Stryder

Students touch a tactile image of sunspots in **Touch the Sun** as part of a solar week event.

Consider offering tactile images for people who are sighted to touch while simultaneously looking through the telescope. At Western Connecticut State University, Dr. Dennis Dawson has tactile images available right in the dome. As visitors touch the image, they say it helps them to focus on particular features of the object seen in the eyepiece.

Visitors at the Western Connecticut State University Observatory touch a tactile image of the Orion Nebula while viewing it through the telescope.

Making Touchable Images during a Star Party

Touchable images allow people who are blind to see a picture with their fingertips and mind's eye. Although the tactile images created in

Braille books take time to manufacture, you can create nearly real-time images at your observing session if you have the right equipment.

You need a way to save a telescopic image into a digital file format, like JPEG, and a computer with a program that allows you to make some simple image adjustments. You also need a black and white printer (in this case, a laser printer works better than inkjet), a photocopy machine, a thermal expansion machine and swell paper (Swell Touch is a well-known brand of swell paper). You can do a web search for <swell paper expansion machines> to research the subject. Swell Form (www.americanthermoform. com) and Picture in a Flash (www.humanware. com) are popular brands.

If you don't already have a digital camera, you do not need to purchase a super-expensive model. It is possible to use a digital camera held to the eyepiece, or even an inexpensive web cam mounted to the eyepiece.

Equipment setup for making
real-time tactile images from the telescope:
thermal expansion machine, computer, and printer

Your equipment setup should be kept inside,
away from fluctuations in temperature and
humidity that can affect swell paper. Once you
have captured the digital image, transfer it to
the computer and use a program like Adobe
Photoshop Elements to invert the image so
the object is black and the background (sky)
is white. This is very important! Next, try
adjusting the contrast so there are sharp black
and white boundaries as opposed to gray areas.

Print out your image with the computer's
printer onto regular copy paper. Then,
photocopy this image onto the swell paper.
Finally, run the swell paper page through the

thermal expansion machine. There is a special coating on swell paper that, when heated by the thermal expansion machine, causes areas that are black on the page to puff up. The resulting page is a touchable version of the telescopic image, ready to be explored!

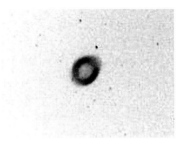

Westminster Astronomical Society

Original Image recorded from the telescope

Image processed, cropped and ready for tactile printing

Westminster Astronomical Society

The author has just created a tactile image for a star party at Johns Hopkins University.

Handling Tactile Images

Here are some things you and your visitors should know about handling tactile images made with swell paper. Swell paper images can last dozens of touch readings if these simple guidelines are followed.

- Be sure that your hands are clean and dry when you handle the images. Dampness can damage the raised textures.
- With fingertips, lightly trace the tactile textures. Never push down on the textures, as they are fragile.
- Examine tactile images on a solid surface like a table or clipboard. This helps prevent any creases or tears.
- Never store tactile images face to face, because the textures can rub off.

I like to slide tactile images into page protectors so that the textures are still legible by touch but also protected for longer use.

I also keep a file of the processed images so I can reprint new tactile images when the original ones become worn and need to be replaced.

If you are thinking, "this sounds like a lot of work," that isn't true. With an efficient setup, you can produce a tactile telescopic image in less than five minutes after the original image is captured. That's not a bad turnaround time, and the response of people to touchable images is magical!

Andy Cheng, Texas Astronomical Society of Dallas

A star party participant explores a tactile image with a member of the Texas Astronomical Society of Dallas.

If you are thinking, "I'm not going to all that trouble because we never have people who are blind attending," then you should know this. According to the Braille Institute in Los Angeles, there are an estimated 15 million people who are blind or visually impaired in the United States. Just because a person who is blind has not attended your educational program, this is no reason to assume they will not in the future.

Be proactive! Plan to make telescope images accessible from the start. And don't think tactile images are only for participants who are blind or visually impaired. Making something accessible to a person with a disability also makes it more accessible for others. People who are sighted, especially children, also enjoy and benefit from touching an image as they take another peek through the telescope. Your work is never without merit.

Enlarging the Image

A video camera can be connected to the eyepiece to broadcast a larger view to a monitor. This is useful for people who cannot climb stairs but still want to see the image from the telescope. The enlarged image can also aid people with low vision.

You can also hold a video camera up to the eyepiece to record and later play back a telescopic image. Objects like the Moon are big, bright, and easy to record with a handheld video camera. The cost of video cameras has dropped considerably, so either technique should fit your budget.

Words Can Create a Picture

As I write these words, I am sitting in front of my computer, choreographing my thoughts in a symphony. My fingers dance along the computer keyboard, and letters appear on my Mac computer monitor. My desk is cluttered with notes, a calculator, pens, and a pile of books. To my right is a wooden lamp with a calico-patterned lampshade. When I look straight beyond my computer, I see various diplomas on the lavender-and-white walls of my home office. On the bookshelves are books and magazines, piles of papers, some models, and some awards.

You've never been to my office, but from this description your mind has painted a picture of what you think it looks like. You have an image in your mind's eye.

Whether you are looking at the Moon through a telescope or a painting in an art gallery, you can describe the characteristics of what you see and share it with others.

Imagine that a friend calls you on the phone and says, "I just saw the most amazing car." What kind of picture does this information give you?

Now rewind that phone call, and have your friend describe how "the roof folded into three sections and slid right into the trunk!" The more objective and descriptive information you include, the better the listener will be able to form a mental image of the object.

Pictorial description helps a person who cannot see the image to imagine it.

Descriptive narration is also beneficial to sighted participants because it can draw their attention to features that they may not have noticed. For example, when people look at Saturn for the first time through a telescope, they are often drawn to the rings as the dominant feature. However, if you tell them to also look at the "star" usually visible near Saturn, you are adding the moon Titan to their experience.

SPOTLIGHT
The Pomona Valley Amateur Astronomers
Pomona, California

In 2004, the Pomona Valley Amateur Astronomers (PVAA) created Project Bright Sky to make astronomy more accessible to people with visual impairments. They teamed up with several Braille Institute locations throughout southern California as well as the Junior Blind of America. Every year they conduct star parties for people with visual disabilities. They also have volunteer teachers available and conduct tactile astronomy classes at the Braille institutes.

Their services, which are free of charge, are a collaborative effort of several amateur astronomy clubs in California. The PVAA star parties are conducted in semi-remote desert environments as well as in the city. The desert events include a ranger-led hike and a sunset dinner followed by an evening of observing bright sky objects in a dark desert sky, far from city lights. As part of their hands-on resources, they bring my tactile books, which, according to the organization "are a huge hit at our events, as we have attendees who are legally blind, totally blind, and sighted."

The light gathering capabilities of telescopes have proven to be tremendous to people attending the PVAA star parties who have some remaining vision. Some participants have been brought to tears when observing the Moon, which up until that night had only been a bright white light; yet now they were seeing its mountains and craters. Digital and astronomical video cameras attached to some of their telescopes provide stunning live images that are transmitted to 12-inch black and white TV monitors. A person who is legally blind can position their eyes as close as needed to the bright astronomical objects on the TV screen. Some have been able to see the dust lanes in the Sombrero Galaxy while observing in a city environment.

Individuals who are totally blind attend their star parties and listen to the telescope operators as they vividly describe what others are seeing through the telescopes or on a TV monitor. The star parties and classroom sessions bring everyone a bit closer to the beautiful and mysterious universe in which we all are observers, regardless of our vision acuity.

The Pomona Valley Amateur Astronomers conduct three to five star parties a year for individuals with vision disabilities. In the past they have conducted astronomy classes at the Orange County Braille Institute in Anaheim, California. The best way to contact them is via email at info@pvaa.us or through their website, www.pvaa.us. When emailing them, be sure to reference Project Bright Sky in the subject line. They work with individuals of any age.

Chapter 3

Invisible and Neurological Disorders

Star parties and other educational programs attract a wide variety of people. You may be able to quickly identify a person with mobility impairment because they are using a wheelchair or electric scooter. A person who is visually impaired may have a cane or guide dog. You may identify a person who is hearing impaired as they sign to a friend. But there is another group of people who have special needs. These are people with non-obvious (invisible) disabilities.

Invisible Disabilities

Learning disabilities can affect how a person internalizes, processes, and responds to new information through reading, writing, and listening. It can also hinder a person's ability to reason and determine the answers to math problems. Of all the disabilities identified in schools, learning disabilities have the highest incidence.

A learning disability does not mean that the person has below-average intelligence. The person may have average or above-average intelligence but have difficulties in learning specific tasks. For example, a person with dyslexia may have difficulty reading, while someone with dysgraphia may have difficulty in writing. While it is easy to identify a person using an assistive mobility device, it can be hard to quickly identify a person who has a learning disability outside the classroom. Therefore, it is very helpful to provide information, activities and instructions in a multi-modal format. For example, if you display or project pictures, add short informational captions with easy-to-understand vocabulary that help explain the images. Teach concepts through songs and kinesthetic activities. Offer hands-on activities that help visitors discover through experiment and inquiry. Using a variety of strategies increases the opportunity to actively engage people through their personal strengths.

Learning disability is not the only kind of invisible disability. Some students have emotional disturbance, with outbursts resulting from difficulties interacting in social situations. The inability of a person to contain emotions can hinder their academic learning.

Students may have difficulty being understood because of impediments in articulation or flow of speech (stuttering). Students may also have challenges in understanding instructions presented verbally. For example, people who have difficulty concentrating may have attention deficit hyperactivity disorder (ADHD), epilepsy, or traumatic brain injury.

Traumatic brain injury is the most common cause of acquired disability for children. It happens when there is injury to the head that may have included a loss of consciousness. Among the ways traumatic brain injury can happen are falls from playground equipment, the blunt force of a car or bicycle accident, and injuries sustained from child abuse. Traumatic brain injury can cause changes in personality, loss of already-acquired knowledge, and impairment of new learning. According to the Centers for Disease Control and Prevention (CDC), 1.7 million people sustain traumatic brain injuries each year.

Chronic illness is also an invisible disability. People may have fatigue, muscle pain, or bone pain. Diabetes, chronic fatigue syndrome, arthritis, cancer, sickle-cell disease, and Lyme disease are examples of chronic illness. They can affect a person's health and stamina. You can help by having some chairs nearby that people can use to rest on and accessible, level parking that is close to the observing site. Available water and an accessible restroom may be necessities for some participants.

Many people have chemical sensitivities, such as to perfume or incense. Visitors with allergies and asthma may have adverse reactions to strong odors. For everyone's comfort, make your educational event a fragrance-free zone.

Autism Spectrum Disorders

Autism spectrum disorders (ASD) are a collection of developmental disabilities of the brain that can cause impairment of social interaction and communication, as well as fixation on activities and interests. The impairment covers a broad range of abilities, so it is often referred to as autism spectrum rather than just autism. For example, one person on the autism spectrum may have intellectual disability and also not be able to communicate verbally, yet another person on the autism spectrum may be completely verbal and have a high capacity in a particular subject, such as math, science, or engineering. Think of ASD as a continuum of abilities and challenges.

According to the revised 2012 CDC statistics, about 1 out of every 88 children in the United

States has autism spectrum disorder. Chances are very high that a person on the autism spectrum will attend one of your educational programs.

Some people on the autism spectrum are highly intelligent and can communicate verbally. Other people may have intellectual disabilities or may communicate nonverbally, possibly through the use of an iPad. And some people can make eye contact or listen to information but not do both simultaneously.

Dr. Temple Grandin is an expert in animal behavior. She is also a noted speaker and bestselling author on autism spectrum disorder. Grandin has a personal understanding of ASD because she is on the autism spectrum. In her book **The Way I See It**, Dr. Grandin suggests a link between autism spectrum disorder genetics and genius. She speculates, "Isaac Newton, Thomas Jefferson, Socrates, Lewis Carroll, and Andy Warhol may have been on the autism spectrum." In fact, she writes, "If Albert Einstein were born today, he would be diagnosed with autism. He had no speech until age three, obsessively repeated certain sentences until age seven, and spent hours building houses from playing cards. His social skills remained odd through most of his life."

How can you identify a person on the autism spectrum? Individuals with ASD share some common characteristics. They often have difficulty with social interaction. Many people will avoid eye contact or not be able to understand facial expressions. They may have trouble learning to take turns in a conversation. Simply getting along with others can be challenging for a person with ASD.

Some people with ASD have extreme sensitivity to light, sound, or touch. One person may be overwhelmed by too many visual images. The conversations of a crowd of people can be overstimulating to a second person. A piece of clothing may be extremely irritating to another person. The smell of perfume, or odors presented in a 4D movie experience, may be overwhelming for another. For many, experiencing these sensitivities and not being able to communicate verbally can create frustration and increased stress levels quickly, leading to a behavioral outburst. This may include unusual vocal sounds or physical movements that others may find upsetting or annoying.

Being on the autism spectrum means that visitors to your programs and facilities will have different needs and abilities. However, you can help make their experience enjoyable by planning ahead.

Create material that families can review before arriving at your program or facility. For example, design a "what to expect" storyboard with words and pictures that describe a typical museum, planetarium, or observatory experience. This planning can help a visitor on the autism spectrum feel prepared and in control.

Museums and exhibitions in general can be overstimulating because there is a lot to see and do. Consider providing a non-crowded, quiet, "judgment free" area with less stimulation; and consider offering times when visitors can interact with participatory exhibits at their own pace. Use of colorful graphics and less text can be helpful. Avoid bright, contrasting colors that may be too stimulating for some eyes. The flicker of fluorescent lights may be stressful for certain individuals. Avoid loud sounds, such as the ringing of bells or the scraping sounds of moving furniture across uncarpeted floors, as they may be painful for some ears.

If you offer lectures, planetarium shows, or films, leave a back door open so families can come and go as needed. This relieves stress and puts control with visitors.

Transitions can be another source of stress for people with ASD. Standing in a long line, and getting up and leaving after a presentation can be challenging for some. To relieve some of this stress, you might consider offering early admission and a special entrance that bypasses a long line.

Explain the layout and schedule of your event. For example, "Everyone is invited to the auditorium to learn about the Moon. After the slide show, telescopes will be available for everyone to view the Moon's craters."

Lessons from Educators on Providing Experiences for People on the Autism Spectrum

The following two interviews describe specific accommodations made in a planetarium and accommodations made in a children's museum that has a strong science focus. Both educators share their experiences in creating welcoming and accessible opportunities for people with ASD.

Interview 1: Jerry Vinski

Jerry Vinski is Director of the Raritan Valley Community College Reeve Planetarium in New Jersey. The RVCC Planetarium presents a planetarium show specifically designed for visitors on the autism spectrum. In this interview, Jerry explains how this planetarium show for children on the autism spectrum was created and describes his experience in working with people who have ASD.

Cathy Vinski

Jerry Vinski

I. How did you first get involved with doing a show for people on the autism spectrum?

My wife is a speech therapist and works with children with autism. After seeing an article in the local newspaper about a play at a local stage theater for children with autism, she convinced me there was a need to create a planetarium show for this population.

A local movie theater has also set aside a time for a special "autism showing" of a new release. Because of state education requirements, we have seen an increase in groups with disabilities visiting our planetarium. When talking to the teachers we became aware that they left some students behind because of behavioral issues. This was a fact that my wife confirmed. There is a population on the autism spectrum that often acts out and disturbs others easily. We are specifically trying to reach out to children that typically do not attend public events. We are trying to make our show a family affair.

2. How did you learn about autism spectrum?

We have reached out to autism groups to help advertise the program. We also have their literature available on a resource table for the families attending. In New Jersey we have several school and resource centers for autism, such as Autism Speaks, Autism New Jersey, Parents of Autistic Children (POAC), The Autism Think Tank, Eden Institute, Rutgers Developmental Center, Midland School, and Methany School, to name a few.

3. **How did you decide how to structure the show to best meet the needs of people on the autism spectrum?**

Both the movie and stage theaters did not change their performances. They did the same show that they would do for any group. To make it more autistic friendly they left a door open, with lights on dim, and made sure the sound did not startle anyone. The RVCC Planetarium experience takes that into consideration also, but we include specific segments in our show that are the types of visuals and music that children on the autism spectrum enjoy.

4. **How is the planetarium show structured? How much narration versus visuals?**

The show includes a variety of space video songs, constellations, laser songs, and an 8-minute full dome show about shapes in space that asks the question, Is it round like a pancake or round like a ball? (Planets are round like a ball but they orbit like a pancake.) Since the show is made up of about a dozen segments, it is easy to replace any part with the creation of a new song and visuals. Over a period of months the show evolves into a different show from the original.

Laser songs have a nonstop visual aspect to them, with kites, words, and numbers covering the dome in laser light and in video images. Lasers sometimes have a flicker effect to them, so we do the laser songs last. The last two songs or so are something to appeal more to adults, such as music by the Beatles.

Music is the basis for the show because children with autism tend to enjoy it so much. Many visuals are used, as this holds children's attention and keeps them stimulated along with the music. In our experience the children have made it through the entire program, which lasts over 45 minutes. Many families have visited multiple times, and they are all extremely appreciative for having the experience available for their child. If a child with a condition on the autism spectrum can sit through and enjoy a typical movie in the local theater, then this planetarium program is not for them.

5. Did you make any modifications visually to the show?

I would say the entire show is modified and not like any other show that we have. I would not show this program to a typically developing child the way we present it. It is not a story to follow, and we are not trying to teach them anything as formal as moon phases, for example. Each child will retain something different from the experience with the idea that multiple visits will expand on that knowledge. On each visit they will absorb a bit more of the visuals and words.

6. Did you make any modifications to the audio track of the show?

The audio level is at an average level. We took care that the audio for each segment faded in very slowly to a comfortable level.

No sudden loud starts to a song. If a normal song fades in over 1 or 2 seconds, ours fade in over 4 or 6 seconds.

7. Do you plan to continue offering these special shows?

Yes we plan on offering this experience monthly.   www.raritanval.edu/planetarium has details.

8. How successful have these shown been with the audience?

These shows have been extremely well received by both the parents and the children. The age range has been quite large, the youngest visitor being about 4 years old and the oldest being late teens. Most are between 8 and 12. The parents have been very grateful that we are offering this program. These families would not normally visit the regular public RVCC Planetarium shows. Most parents would say that the show kept their child engaged. Many commented that 5 to 10 minutes is often all their child will do before they start to get frustrated with an activity and need to move on. All of the children lasted for over 45 minutes in this show.

9. **What advice would you give to other planetarium and astronomy educators who may work with visitors on the autism spectrum? What works and what should be avoided?**

Music keeps this audience engaged. Talking, as would be done in a typical "Night Sky" show does not hold their attention. They will start to get frustrated and act out in a behavior that is disturbing to a non-autistic audience. New Jersey is a densely populated state and has a large population of children with autism. As the term implies, autism spectrum is a range of abilities and issues. The parents of these children do not often attend public programs or even a nice dinner out as a family. If they do, they are aware that they may need to truncate their visit due to their child's behavior. They are trying to give their child all of the educational experiences that they can, and the majority of the time they do this without support from others. At RVCC, we are trying to reach the families with children that do not often attend public events. The RVCC Reeve Planetarium is providing a judgment-free environment for these families to experience a planetarium show that will engage their children.

Interview 2: Amy Spencer

Amy Spencer is Director of Early Childhood Education and Parent Resources at the Discovery Museums in Acton, Massachusetts. She oversees all early childhood public program and exhibit initiatives and community outreach programs tailored to underserved audiences. In this interview, Amy shares her experience in the Especially for Me program for families with children on the autism spectrum and families with infants and

Ann Sgarzi, Discovery Museums

Amy Spencer

toddlers with hearing loss at the Discovery Museums.

I. Can you tell me a little about the Discovery Museums in Acton? What kinds of exhibits and programs do visitors experience?

The Discovery Museums were founded in 1982. Our mission is to inspire enduring curiosity and love of learning through interactive discovery, hands-on inquiry, and scientific investigation. We are a children's museum with a strong program in science, but our goal is to provide interdisciplinary experiences in the arts, sciences, and humanities. The cornerstone of our educational philosophy is to provide a safe, stimulating environment that fosters creativity and curiosity while inspiring a lifelong love of learning. Our 4.5-acre campus includes two buildings: a cozy children's building with imaginative learning spaces and a science building that presents basic science principles using familiar objects.

2. Who is the main audience at the Discovery Museums?

We serve 165,000 visitors annually. Over 16,000 school children visit our campus annually. Our Traveling Science Workshops reach an additional 24,000 students in 1,100 classrooms per year. Our 1,900 member families come from more than 175 towns and represent the rich ethnic diversity of the region. We offer special programs to reach underserved populations, with 21 percent of our audience attending for free or reduced admissions.

3. What is the Especially For Me program?

In 2010, we launched a program called Especially for Me: Expanding Access to Museum Fun for All Families, with the Autism Alliance of MetroWest and the Deaf and Hard of Hearing Program of the Children's Hospital Boston at Waltham. The goal of the program is to better serve families in the MetroWest and surrounding communities in Massachusetts with children on the autism spectrum or deaf or hard of hearing children.

Ours is one of two children's museums in New England who have formal programs to support families with children on the autism spectrum by providing them with regular free events during non-public hours, to accommodate their unique customer service and learning needs. Uniquely in New England we have a formal program that collaborates with a prestigious hospital to support families with deaf or hard of hearing children by providing them with regular free events during non-public hours to enhance the language acquisition of infants and toddlers using trained language facilitators and ASL interpreters and to accommodate the unique customer service and learning needs of children of all ages with hearing loss. In 2011, we hosted six free events that served over 750 people. Due to the growing success of the program, we will host twelve events (six for each audience) in 2012, with a goal of serving 1500 people.

4. How did you get involved in working with children on the autism spectrum? Did a person or organization contact you?

The Autism Alliance of MetroWest has organized annual family nights at the Discovery Museums for years. When I took over the museum rentals program in 2010, I proposed to the heads of both organizations that we should take over responsibility for the events, as it should be a part of its mission to reach out to underserved audiences. We started out with two evening events in 2010, grew to four events in 2011, and have six events scheduled for 2012. The number of events has increased annually to help meet the public demand for the events.

5. What were your expectations of creating a program for visitors on the autism spectrum?

My expectations for the program were to provide special evenings for families with children on the autism spectrum to visit the Discovery Museums, to accommodate the children's sensitivities to crowds and noise, and provide opportunities for the parents to network with similar parents. Though these events are scheduled during non-public times, it is our hope that these events provide a gateway, so families can work towards visiting us during public hours.

6. Did you make any modifications to the programs or environment for visitors on the autism spectrum?

We decided not to make any changes to the exhibits because all of the experiences are hands-on and open-ended, so already appropriate for this audience. To prepare for these events, we trained our staff in what autism is and is not and ways to support the customer service and education needs of this audience.

7. **What have your experiences been with visitors on the autism spectrum?** Though our events have been well attended, the number of visitors and amount of noise have not been too much for the parents and children to handle. The general consensus we hear from parents is that they don't worry if the children become over-stimulated and act out, because they are in a non-judgmental environment. Since autism is invisible, parents are often labeled as "bad parents" when their children on the autism spectrum display behaviors that are deemed inappropriate by other adults who know nothing about the families' circumstances. Parents are grateful for these events, which allow them to be themselves and bond as an entire family.

8. What most surprised you about offering programs for visitors on the autism spectrum?

I have been most surprised by the parents' gratitude for the events and the importance of the free admission. Parents continually express their gratefulness for the events and how rare it is for them to find other community activities that are as welcoming to them. I have had parents cry and hug me to express their appreciation for the program. Parents have also shared that the free admission for the events is important because when they attend an activity there is never any way to predict how long they are going to be able to attend. They could spend over $100 to attend an activity only to have to leave after five minutes because of how their child on the spectrum is feeling. Having free admission takes away the risk of losing precious family funds that are already limited due to the expenses required to care for a child on the autism spectrum.

9. How has the overall response been for these programs?

The public's response to the program has been very positive. Generally, 150 to 200 people attend the events, and we regularly need to close our event registration period early due to registration becoming full.

10. What advice do you have for any museum or science educator on best practices for interacting with and creating programs for visitors on the autism spectrum?

It is important to collaborate with organizations that support families with children on the autism spectrum to better understand what autism is and is not and learn how to support the customer service and education needs of this audience. If the museum already provides hands-on, open-ended exhibits, then it already has the type of activities that are best suited for this audience. It is important that the staff be trained on how to support the customer service and education needs of visitors on the autism spectrum, so they have the confidence and the skill to enrich the families' museum experience.

Chapter 4

Augmentative and Alternative Communication

You are driving toward an intersection when you see a red light. You bring your car to a stop and wait until the light turns green. You and other drivers understand that the color and location of the light on the traffic signal indicate when it is safe to travel or when you need to stop and wait.

You read a magazine ad for a new travel destination. Images of smiling children and families fill the page. Even before you read the accompanying text, you recognize these pictures as conveying facial expressions and body language of happiness. The advertiser is saying that you too could be that happy if you took that trip.

Now imagine that you take a trip to Athens, Greece, to celebrate a special occasion. After several hours of visiting a museum, you need to use the bathroom. You look for the "restrooms" sign in the museum but do not find it. "It's got to be somewhere!" you think, as your situation gets more urgent. Finally you realize that you have seen several signs that say "WC," and learn that in Athens, the toilet is called the water closet.

Behind the counter in many fast food restaurants is a menu of items along with a pictorial display of the combination or value meals. How many times have you heard other customers say, "I'll have the number one meal" and you understood exactly what food was in their order? If you didn't speak the local language, or could not speak at all, you could still point to the picture of the food you wanted, and the clerk would understand your order.

Television commercials often have 30 seconds or less to promote the benefits of their product. They use clever words, logos, color combinations, and images to make you remember it. Commercials are repeated during the viewing day and also pop up on internet sites. Before you know it, you have been trained to recognize the product. This also applies to political advertising around election time, where repeated TV ads, postcard mailings, and telephone calls bombard you with information and rhetoric about the candidates.

Advertisers, engineers, city planners, and people working in customer service understand that nonverbal communication is concise and powerful. Augmentative and alternative communication (AAC) encompasses a variety of techniques for a person to communicate nonverbally. Rather than using a paragraph to describe an idea, people can learn to recognize one word, a symbol, or a specific type of picture as a definition. This is important, because not all people are able to use speech for communication.

Autism spectrum disorder, speech impediment, and cerebral palsy are examples of disabilities that may prevent or cause difficulties with speech or understanding a person's speech. Stroke and other brain injuries can also leave a person without the ability to speak or communicate verbally. This does not mean that the person cannot understand and process information; rather, it means that he or she must use strategies other than speech to communicate with others.

If you are a person who communicates verbally, you may naturally combine facial expressions and hand gestures as you talk. But if the person with whom you are communicating cannot respond verbally, it is important to have a variety of strategies for mutual expression.

I have a friend who has two sons on the autism spectrum. When they are out on errands and a son needs to use a restroom, he points to a picture of a toilet to let her know. When they are out shopping, her sons know what products they like because they recognize the packaging.

In some special education classrooms, instructors may use a combination of the written word, spoken word, and sign language to communicate with students. For example, the teachers may greet the students by speaking "good morning" while presenting the sign language gesture for "good morning" and then pointing to "good morning" as words written on a sign or blackboard. The combination of several communication techniques allows them to reach more students than with one method.

How will you communicate with a person who cannot respond verbally? Do not panic or be nervous. You can communicate using different strategies; and these include speaking, facial and body gestures, and pictures.

How will you understand what the person who does not respond verbally has to say? Many people use a combination of pictures and words, called a communication or picture board, as a tool for communicating. The person may use a finger to point to a specific picture, word, or combination of words.

Communication Boards

The communication board may be a simple (non-electronic) picture board, where the person points to specific areas on the board to convey an intention or idea. Electronic picture boards interact with the user; when the user presses a picture or word, the device may speak or even perform a logical **branch** to jump to a completely new set of pictures and words.

Several companies sell electronic picture boards on which the user touches an illustration or text

DynaVox Mayer-Johnson, www.dynavoxtech.com

The DynaVox Maestro communication board

on part of the screen to relay their desires and responses. For example, the person may press a picture of a person smiling to indicate that they are happy. Or, they may press an image of a cup to request a beverage. These devices can verbalize the image or combine text phrases for extended vocabulary.

You may also encounter a person using a communication application called Proloquo2Go

AssistiveWare

The Proloquo2Go main screen

on an iPhone, iPod Touch, or iPad. This interactive program gives children and adults who are not able to speak the ability to communicate with others. Text can be displayed as both letters and pictures so the user can press what they want to say and have the device speak the words. It's a clever and useful program.

You can create your own simple communication board, geared toward your educational program, and have it available as needed. Use a computer program, such as Microsoft PowerPoint, to design and organize the images (for example, Moon, Jupiter, Saturn) or particular vocabulary words you expect to use at the event.

Your communication board may include a question or statement and a series of responses. For anyone participating in a star party, you would probably want your communication board to include images of the types of objects that you will be viewing. You might even want to ask visitors if they would like to choose an object to see with the telescope.

You may want to include follow-up questions and statements such as these:

- Which object would you like to view with the telescope?
- Would you like to know more about this object?
- Would you like to view another object with the telescope?
- May I show you how this telescope works?

The communication board can help foster dialog between a person who communicates verbally and a person who uses alternative communication through pictures.

Chapter 5

Communicating with Visitors Who Are Deaf or Hard of Hearing

According to Gallaudet University demographic surveys (1997–2003), an estimated 13 percent of the U.S. population has hearing problems. Children make up the smallest percentage of this group, but of people 65 and older, more than 29 percent report severe hearing difficulties.

People who are hearing impaired may use a portable volume amplification device or they may use hearing aids. And like some people who are deaf, they may also lip read. For everyone's benefit, you should always face the person you are speaking to and keep your hands and objects away from your mouth. Speak clearly and do not shout. If the person with hearing loss needs you to repeat the information, they will let you know. If unsure you can politely ask them. But never automatically assume that anyone lip reads.

Estimates vary on exactly how many people use American Sign Language (ASL) as their primary mode of communication. Some studies suggest that ASL is the fourth most used language in the United States. (Many countries have their own particular sign language. ASL is used in the U.S.) Those communicating in ASL include people with hearing impairments, along with their friends, families, and teachers, and also people who do not communicate orally because of disabilities such as autism spectrum disorder. Chances are high that you will encounter a person who communicates with ASL at your astronomy program.

ASL does not have the same grammatical structure as spoken or signed English. (Signed

English is a direct translation of spoken English and may be used by people who had hearing earlier in their lives.) This means that a student who is deaf and communicates primarily through ASL may be reading written English at a lower grade level than other students of their age.

If you provide text captions and labels for exhibits and programming, it may be helpful to present a form of this information at grade 3 to 5 reading level. This is also helpful for visitors who are learning English as a second language.

If you are an astronomy educator who presents a live talk before telescopic viewing, create an informational page to accompany your talk. If you present a planetarium show, create a script that a person could review before, or take away after, the show. These types of documents will help more people understand and enjoy your presentation.

Do you provide a tour of your museum or observatory? You may find yourself interpreting an exhibition for a group, accompanied by a sign language interpreter. When this happens, be sure to insert pauses in your presentation to allow the interpreter enough time to interpret what you are saying. Extra time needs to be built into the tour so that the interpreter is able to stand next to the tour guide while having the attention of all those in attendance.

Suppose that a visitor who communicates with ASL has questions and no one is available to interpret. How will you communicate?

One suggestion is to always have paper and pen handy so that you can communicate through the written word. The person can ask questions and you can answer them.

Do you have a smart phone? In a pinch, you can use your cell phone as a mini-keyboard. You can make the words easier to read if you have a larger screen, say an electronic tablet like an iPad, or an extra laptop available.

Be proactive and learn a few signs, especially those words that you will use often, such as

Sun, Moon, star, planet, galaxy, and telescope. You can download an application from iTunes to help you learn ASL. iSign is a program for the iPhone, iPod Touch, and iPad that can help you learn individual signs. iSign has an animated ASL dictionary with an avatar that demonstrates the signs through gesture. Choose a text word from the dictionary, and the avatar will show you how to sign it. The program contains 800 signs that can be sorted alphabetically or categorically. It's handy to have!

If you are presenting a PowerPoint slide show, insert descriptive captions in each slide to complement your talk. If you are showing an astronomy video, consider showing a version with captions. Captions are great for people who can't hear the audio and are helpful for people who speak English as a second language.

SPOTLIGHT
Accessible Astronomy Programs
for Students at Yerkes Observatory
Williams Bay, Wisconsin

Vivian Hoette is an astronomy educator at Yerkes Observatory in Wisconsin. But, before coming to Yerkes, Vivian taught students in preschool through high school as a formal science education teacher for 20 years. Then she began her second career as an informal science educator in the mid-1990s at the Adler Planetarium & Astronomy Museum in Chicago.

Richard Dreiser
Vivian Hoette

Vivian's interest in astronomy coincided with the last approach of Comet Halley. She was teaching middle school and wanted to show her students a close-up view of the comet. But all the observing sessions scheduled with the local astronomy clubs were clouded out, so she got a star map and learned her way around the night sky. Armed with a pair of binoculars, Vivian invited her students to view Comet Halley on some very cold winter nights. She had so much fun that she was hooked!

At Yerkes Observatory, Vivian began working with students with disabilities. Using the Braille book **Touch the Universe** as a springboard, she invited students who were blind to participate in a weeklong program of hands-on astronomy activities. Years later, some of those same students came back to work with Vivian as hired staff assistants. Together, they developed new tactile materials and programs that have been attended by students who are blind and students who are deaf.

Vivian has made it a personal mission to incorporate diversity into her work and into the operations of Yerkes Observatory. She has collaborated with staff and students from the Wisconsin School for the Deaf (WSD) on several projects. For example, a student intern from WSD has been working with one of the Yerkes scientists on researching and analyzing suspected variable stars on historical glass plates. Yerkes Observatory has also sponsored a number of students from WSD at national astronomy conferences. These opportunities combine the highly specialized work at Yerkes with individually designed education of students at the Wisconsin School for the Deaf.

Sign-language interpreters have been provided at workshops, star parties, and group tour at Yerkes Observatory.

College students who are blind or have low vision have also actively participated in programs at Yerkes Observatory. The Yerkes staff and interns, notably Katherine Watson, play an essential role in developing and testing the Braille title font, tactile image textures, and accompanying audio description for the Space Telescope Science Institute's Amazing Space tactile-astronomy Hubble image releases.

Vivian Hoette

Elementary school students from the Wisconsin School for the Deaf learn about an instrument being built at Yerkes for the Stratospheric Observatory for Infrared Astronomy (SOFIA).

Are there areas of astronomy that can't be made accessible? Vivian doesn't think so. She advises anyone thinking about developing programs for disabled students to partner with the schools or programs that serve those communities. Some teachers in schools may discourage students with disabilities from considering science as a career because it is inaccessible. She says, "Science can be accessible. It is my hope that through collaborations such as those at Yerkes, students who are deaf will help make new contributions in the field of astronomy."

Chapter 6

Service Animals

It is not uncommon for people to be accompanied by service animals. The Americans with Disabilities Act (ADA) was updated and, starting in 2011, defines a service animal as a dog that is individually trained to do work or perform tasks for a person with a disability. According to the ADA revised definition, service animals perform some of the functions and tasks that individuals with a disability cannot perform themselves. Examples of such work or tasks include guiding people who are blind, alerting people who are deaf, pulling a wheelchair, alerting and protecting a person who is having a seizure, reminding a person with mental illness to take prescribed medications, or calming a person with post traumatic stress disorder during an anxiety attack.

The work or task a dog has been trained to provide must be directly related to the person's disability. Dogs whose sole function is to provide comfort or emotional support do not qualify as service animals under the ADA.

Service animals are allowed wherever people are allowed. A person with a disability cannot be asked to remove their service animal from the premises unless the dog is out of control and the handler does not take effective action to control it, or the dog is not housebroken. When there is a legitimate reason to ask that a service animal be removed, staff must offer the disabled individual the opportunity to obtain goods or services without the animal's presence.

All service animals are identified by a special leash, harness, or vest. When they are assisting their person, they are working and must not be distracted. Although you may be tempted, please do not pat service animals; they are not pets.

ADA regulations specify what inquiries can be made about service animals. For example, when it is not obvious what service an animal provides, only limited inquiries are allowed. Staff may ask two questions: Is the dog a service animal required because of a disability, and what work or task has the dog been trained to perform? Staff cannot ask about the person's disability, require medical documentation, require a special identification card or training documentation for the dog, or ask that the dog demonstrate its ability to perform the work or task.

Maryanne Melley
Plaza, a guide dog, enjoys a day at the beach.

According to the 2010 ADA regulations, allergies and fear of dogs are not valid reasons for denying access or refusing service to people using service animals. When a person who is allergic to dog dander and a person who uses a service animal must spend time in the same room or facility, they should both be accommodated by assigning them, if possible, to different locations within the room or different rooms in the facility.

Guide dogs are one type of service animal, used by some individuals who are blind. They wear a special harness with a handle that their person holds. Guide dogs are specially trained to respond to certain commands and to disobey those commands in case of danger to the person. Words printed on the harness remind people not to pet a guide dog because it is working.

Guide dogs are not the only animals trained to help a person who is blind safely navigate. There are some trained miniature horses serving the same function. The miniature horses are about two or three feet tall and weigh under 100 pounds. They wear harnesses that identify them as a service animal, wear special shoes, and wear a special bag under their tail, which acts as a diaper.

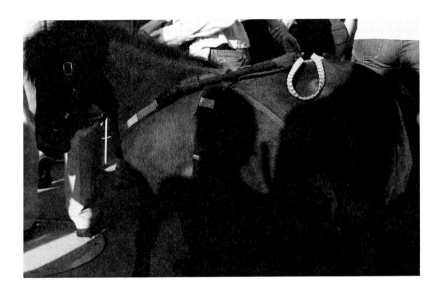

A guide horse in harness

Although dogs are listed specifically as service animals, the revised ADA regulations also include special provisions for miniature horses. The horses should be permitted in any place a service would be permitted if the miniature horse is housebroken; the miniature horse is under the owner's control; the facility can accommodate the miniature horse's type, size, and weight; and the miniature horse's presence will not compromise legitimate safety requirements necessary for safe operation of the facility.

Service animals can also be trained to assist people with other kinds of disabilities in their day-to-day activities, including alerting those with hearing impairments, pulling wheelchairs or carrying and picking up things for people with mobility impairments. They can also help individuals with mobility impairments maintain their balance while walking.

Although you are not legally required to do so, you can assist a service animal by having a bowl and some water available. Service animals get thirsty, too!

Chapter 7

Final Thoughts

Disabilities affect individuals and their friends and families. The CDC estimates that about 1 in 6 children in the U.S. had a developmental disability in 2006–2008, ranging from mild disabilities such as speech and language impairments to serious developmental disabilities, such as intellectual disabilities, cerebral palsy, and autism.

Rather than apologizing or making excuses for why your star party, observatory, science museum, or planetarium is not accessible, try to anticipate the needs of a variety of participants. Do this by planning ahead for the visitor experience through a broad range of learning and experiential methods. Seeing, touching, listening, and talking are strategies to reach a variety of people. Multiple paths of inclusion can make the event accessible to everyone, regardless of any (dis)ability, and can enrich your experience as well.

The accessibility services that you provide for an individual with a disability can affect their families' and friends' decision to visit as a group. Being proactive and creating a welcoming and accessible environment can help your organization open the door to a new population of visitors. It's time to turn on the welcome sign for people of all ability. You can help make science more accessible!

The Ten Commandments of Etiquette for Communicating with People with Disabilities

by National Center for Access Unlimited, Chicago

1. When talking with a person with a disability, speak directly to that person rather than through a companion or sign language interpreter.

2. When introduced to a person with a disability, it is appropriate to offer to shake hands. People with limited hand use or who wear an artificial limb can usually shake hands. (Shaking hands with the left hand is an acceptable greeting.)

3. When meeting a person who is visually impaired, always identify yourself and others who may be with you. When conversing in a group, remember to identify the person to whom you are speaking.

4. If you offer assistance, wait until the offer is accepted. Then listen to or ask for instructions.

5. Treat adults as adults. Address people who have disabilities by their first names only when extending the same familiarity to all others. (Never patronize people who use wheelchairs by patting them on the head or shoulder.)

6. Leaning on or hanging on to a person's wheelchair is similar to leaning on or hanging on to a person and is generally considered annoying. The chair is part of

the personal body space of the person who uses it.

7. Listen attentively when you're talking with a person who has difficulty speaking. Be patient and wait for the person to finish, rather than correcting or speaking for the person. If necessary, ask short questions that require short answers, a nod or shake of the head. Never pretend to understand if you are having difficulty doing so. Instead, repeat what you have understood and allow the person to respond. The response will clue you in and guide your understanding.

8. When speaking with a person who uses a wheelchair or a person who uses crutches, place yourself at eye level in front of the person to facilitate the conversation.

9. To get the attention of a person who is deaf, tap the person on the shoulder or wave your hand. Look directly at the person and speak clearly, slowly, and expressively to determine if the person can read your lips. Not all people who are deaf can read lips. For those who do

lip-read, be sensitive to their needs by placing yourself so that you face the light source and keep hands, cigarettes and food away from your mouth when speaking.

10. Relax. Don't be embarrassed if you happen to use accepted, common expressions such as "See you later," or "Did you hear about that?" that seems to relate to a person's disability. Don't be afraid to ask questions when you're unsure of what to do.

Part II

Guide to Accessible Astronomy Places

The next pages list, alphabetically by state, observatories and planetariums that offer accessible astronomy experiences. Though it may be updated in later editions, I hope this list will disappear, in time, as **all** astronomy places become accessible for everyone.

Please note that the following resource guide and vendor list is for informational purposes only and does not constitute an endorsement of any facility or product by the author. Information was current at press time. For updates on these destinations, please refer to their individual websites.

ALASKA

Thomas Planetarium
Anchorage, Alaska
Features: mobility access

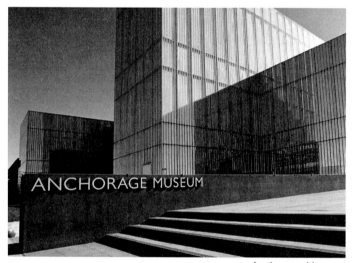

Anchorage Museum

Thomas Planetarium
Anchorage Museum
625 C Street
Anchorage, Alaska 99501
www.anchoragemuseum.org

The Anchorage Museum is home to the Thomas Planetarium. The planetarium has forty-six seats and can accommodate two wheelchairs per show. Planetarium shows are presented on Saturdays and Sundays. A special guided tour of the night sky is presented on the first Friday of each month at 6 p.m. and is followed by two musical laser shows.

Before or after the planetarium show, view astronomy exhibits, including a Moon rock, in Planetarium Hall.

ARIZONA

Lowell Observatory
Flagstaff, Arizona

Features: mobility access, tactile materials, captioning

 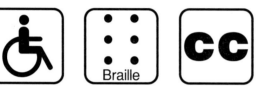

Lowell Observatory

Lowell Observatory
1400 West Mars Hill Road
Flagstaff, Arizona 86001
www.lowell.edu/outreach/hours.php

Lowell Observatory is located at 7,200 feet (2,200 m) in the hills just above Flagstaff, Arizona. Working at this historic site, Clyde Tombaugh discovered Pluto in 1930. The Visitor Center is open daily and features a museum and guided tours. There is a fee for admission. Tactile astronomy materials are available. The Visitor Center and most of the guided tour stops are wheelchair accessible.

The guided tour begins with a captioned video presentation in the auditorium.

Upon leaving the Visitor Center, the tour visits the historic Alvan Clark refractor telescope, where Percival Lowell made observations of the planet Mars. The tour continues to the Rotunda Museum, which features artifacts from Lowell Observatory. The final stop is the telescope with which Pluto was discovered. This stop requires walking up steps to see the telescope.

In the evening, all the buildings used for stargazing are wheelchair accessible, and portable telescopes are available. Check the website for the current schedule.

Kitt Peak National Observatory
Kitt Peak, Arizona
Features: mobility access

Kitt Peak Observatory

Kitt Peak National Observatory
State Road 386
Tohono O'odham Reservation, Arizona
www.noao.edu/outreach/kpvc/plan_trip.html

Kitt Peak National Observatory is about a 90-minute drive from Tucson, Arizona, at an elevation of 6,875 feet (2,100 m). Parking is available near the Visitor Center. Cell phones may not be used at Kitt Peak because they interfere with the two radio telescopes at the observatory. Driving directions to the observatory can be found at: www.noao.edu /outreach/kpvc/Directions.html.

The Kitt Peak Visitor Center is open every day except Thanksgiving Day, Christmas Day, and New Year's Day. Kitt Peak National Observatory has the largest collection of optical research telescopes in the world, and a few are open to the public. During the day, guided one-hour tours of the Mayall 4 m, the 2.1 m, and 2 m McMath-Pierce Solar Telescope (photo), the world's largest solar telescope, are offered daily, but most stops on the tours require climbing stairs. The only accessible part of the guided tour is one level of the McMath-Pierce Solar Telescope. Visitors may also opt to follow the visitor map and take a self-guided tour.

In the evening, Kitt Peak offers a nightly observing program (NOP) with the 20-inch (51 cm) telescope, which is wheelchair accessible. Because of its popularity, you should make reservations for the nightly observing program two to four weeks in advance. On average, 7,000 people a year attend one of these evening programs. If the skies are cloudy, indoor programs and tours are substituted.

For those people who wish to observe all night long, an advanced observing program (AOP) is available.

Audio tours of the 4 m, 2.1 m, and McMath-Pierce Solar Telescopes may be downloaded at: www.noao.edu/outreach/kpvc/mp3/.

ARKANSAS

Donald W. Reynolds Planetarium
Arkadelphia, Arkansas
Features: mobility access

Henderson State University

Donald W. Reynolds Planetarium
Henderson State University
1100 Henderson St.
Arkadelphia, Arkansas 71999
http://www.hsu.edu/interior2.aspx?id=759

The Donald Reynolds Planetarium is located on the first floor of the Reynolds Science Building at Henderson State University. The planetarium is wheelchair accessible and can accommodate two wheelchairs per show.

Public planetarium shows are presented three times a month during the fall and spring semesters. Check the planetarium home page for the current planetarium show schedule.

Weather permitting, stargazing is offered outside, after the planetarium show, with a portable telescope.

University of Central Arkansas Planetarium
Conway, Arkansas

Features: mobility access

University of Central Arkansas

University of Central Arkansas Planetarium
Department of Physics and Astronomy
Lewis Science Center
University of Central Arkansas
Conway, Arkansas 72035
http://faculty.uca.edu/saustin/Astronomy
/planetarium.html

The University of Central Arkansas Planetarium is located in the Lewis Science Center building at UCA–Conway. The science center and planetarium are wheelchair accessible.

The planetarium theater features a 30-foot dome and Spitz 512 star projector. Six wheelchairs can be accommodated in each planetarium show.

During the week, the planetarium is used by the university and as part of field trips for local schools.

Public planetarium shows are presented once a month. These presentations include a tour of the night sky and information on current astronomical events. Check the planetarium home page for the public planetarium show schedule.

CALIFORNIA

Griffith Observatory
Los Angeles, California

Features: mobility access, low vision access, assistive listening access

Griffith Observatory

Griffith Observatory
2800 East Observatory Road
Los Angeles, California 90027
www.griffithobservatory.org

The historic Griffith Observatory opened in 1935 and underwent a $93 million renovation and expansion in 2002. The observatory is located on the southern slope of Mount Hollywood in Griffith Park.

Admission to the observatory building and exhibits is free. There is a fee to attend a planetarium show. Assistive listening headsets are available in the planetarium.

Daytime access to live video of the Sun's image is available in the exhibit hall. An evening video and audio link from the historic observatory to the Wilder Hall of the Eye exhibit area includes video from the telescope eyepiece, video inside the observatory dome, and commentary by the observatory astronomer. Portable telescopes are available on the front observatory lawn.

The Griffith Observatory is open on weekends and most weekdays. Free sky observing is available each evening the Observatory is open and skies are clear. Visitors should check the Griffith Observatory home page for current operating hours.

Chabot Space and Science Center and Observatory
Oakland, California

Features: mobility access, assistive listening access

Chabot Space and Science Center

Chabot Observatory
10000 Skyline Boulevard
Oakland, California 94619
www.chabotspace.org

Wheelchairs are available for use in the Science Center on a first-come, first-served basis.

Wheelchairs may be borrowed at the front desk.

The Chabot Space and Science Center is located in Oakland, California. This educational science center engages visitors with science exhibits, planetarium shows, and large format films.

The Chabot Observatory is located within the science center and boasts the "largest research-quality telescopes open to the public west of the Mississippi." The observatory houses three telescopes, which are all wheelchair accessible. The largest telescope is a 36-inch (91 cm) reflector, named Nellie. This telescope offers visitors a view of the cosmos with an ARE-125 articulated eyepiece.

The domes of the other two telescopes can be entered with a wheelchair, but these telescopes require a visitor to observe from a ladder. The 20-inch (51 cm) Warner and Swasey refractor is called Rachel. It was built and installed in 1915 and refurbished in 2000. The 8-inch (20 cm) telescope is an 1883 Alvan Clark named Leah.

The observatory also offers portable telescopes on the roof, which allows access to visitors in wheelchairs.

The observatory is open and free to the public every Friday and Saturday evening, weather permitting.

The Ask Jeeves Planetarium is wheelchair accessible and can accommodate six wheelchairs per show. The planetarium theater has assistive listening devices available.

Reuben H. Fleet Science Center
San Diego, California

Features: mobility access, assistive listening access, captioning (IMAX films only)

Reuben H. Fleet Science Center

Reuben H. Fleet Science Center
1875 El Prado
San Diego, California 92101
www.rhfleet.org

The Rueben H. Fleet Science Center is located in the Balboa Park section of San Diego, two blocks south of the San Diego Zoo. The Science Center includes includes seven galleries of interactive exhibits and the Heikoff Dome Theater. The Fleet is the first Giant Dome Theater in the country to share a digital planetarium with an IMAX Dome Theater.

The Science Center is wheelchair accessible. Three people in wheelchairs (and their companions) can be accommodated for each show in the Heikoff Dome Theater.

Planetarium shows are presented during the week. A special planetarium show for children is presented each Saturday and Sunday morning. The planetarium and IMAX show schedule is updated on the home page.

Captioning is available for IMAX films. An assistive listening system is available for both IMAX films and planetarium shows. Spanish translation is available for some of the IMAX films and can be heard using an assistive listening headset.

"The Sky Tonight" planetarium show is presented on the first Wednesday of each month. Topics include the current night sky, as seen from San Diego, and other special topics in astronomy. On planetarium show nights, weather permitting, the San Diego Astronomy Association presents the Stars in the Park star party near the Fleet Science Center. A variety of portable telescopes on a paved surface are available for viewing the night sky. The star party is free.

Alexander F. Morrison Planetarium
San Francisco, California

Features: mobility access, assistive listening access, ASL (by advance request)

California Academy of Sciences

Alexander F. Morrison Planetarium
California Academy of Sciences
55 Music Concourse Drive
San Francisco, California 94118
www.calacademy.org/academy/exhibits
/planetarium

The Alexander F. Morrison Planetarium is located in the California Academy of Sciences. The building is wheelchair accessible. A limited number of wheelchairs are available for visitor use on a first-come, first-served basis. Contact a Guest Services staff person upon arrival to borrow a wheelchair.

The Morrison Planetarium is the largest all-digital dome in the world with a 75 foot diameter projection screen tilted at a 30 degree angle. The planetarium has fixed seats at a steep angle. Visitors who have difficulty walking stairs or use wheelchairs should request "wheelchair escort" when show passes are obtained. Six visitors with wheelchairs can be accommodated for each show.

At the end of the show, visitors who are unable to negotiate steps in the planetarium are advised to remain in their seats so they can be escorted out more convenient exits.

An assistive listening system is available in the Morrison Planetarium. Request a volume-adjustable assistive listening system from the Guest Services staff.

The planetarium staff may be able to provide ASL interpretation, but that request must be made three weeks in advance of the visit, to the ADA manager.

COLORADO

Gates Planetarium
Denver, Colorado

Features: mobility access, assistive listening access, captioning

Denver Museum of Nature and Science

Gates Planetarium
Denver Museum of Nature and Science
2001 Colorado Boulevard
Denver, Colorado 80205
www.dmns.org

The Denver Museum of Nature and Science is home to the Gates Planetarium. The Museum is wheelchair accessible; and wheelchairs, canes, and strollers may be borrowed at the information desk. Many of the exhibit areas feature components for people with mobility, hearing, vision, and learning impairments.

The Gates Planetarium is wheelchair accessible but can only fit four wheelchairs per show, on a first-come, first-served basis.

An assistive listening system is available, and assistive listening devices with volume amplification control should be requested either at the box office or from an usher, 20 minutes before show time.

The Planetarium is also equipped with a state-of-the-art Rear Window captioning system that is used for pre-recorded programs. Visitors requiring captioning should request it either at the box office or directly from a planetarium usher.

CONNECTICUT

Western Connecticut State University Observatory
Danbury, Connecticut

Features: mobility access, tactile materials

Western Connecticut State University
Observatory
43 Lake Avenue Extension
Danbury, Connecticut 06811
www.wcsu.edu/starwatch

The Western Connecticut State University Observatory is located on the top of a hill near the Campus Center on the university's Westside Campus. General parking is on University Boulevard; accessible parking for a few cars is located at the top of the hill next to the observatory building.

The observatory houses a 20-inch (51 cm) Ritchey-Chrétien telescope. Visitors must walk up spiral stairs to reach the observatory platform and climb additional steps on a small ladder. Portable telescopes are available for visitors at ground level.

The planetarium theater, located in the observatory building, houses a Spitz A3p star projector and is wheelchair accessible. Two wheelchairs can be accommodated during each planetarium show.

For visually impaired visitors, tactile images are available in the observatory dome and in the planetarium theater. Check the webpage for the planetarium and observing program schedule.

J.J. McCarthy Observatory
New Milford High School
New Milford, Connecticut

Features: mobility access, low vision access

McCarthy Observatory

New Milford High School
388 Danbury Road
New Milford, Connecticut 06776
www.mccarthyobservatory.org

The McCarthy Observatory, located on the campus of New Milford High School in New

Milford, Connecticut, opened in 2000. The facility includes a 16-inch (41 cm) Meade LX200 reflector, a 4.2-inch (10 cm) Takahashi refractor, and several other telescopes.

A public open house is held every second Saturday of the month and there is never a charge to visitors. Check the website for further information.

During daytime hours, a 5-inch (13 cm) Meade refractor and a 3.5-inch (9 cm) Coronado telescope with hydrogen alpha filter provide spectacular views of the Sun. There is no charge to use the observatory.

A custom-made extended eyepiece allows visitors who use wheelchairs or have other mobility challenges the opportunity to view through the main telescope. The McCarthy Observatory is described on pages 7 and 8.

Check the website for current observing schedule.

DISTRICT OF COLUMBIA

National Air and Space Museum Observatory
Washington, D.C.

Features: mobility access, low vision access; assistive listening access and captioning (planetarium only)

Smithsonian National Air and Space Museum

National Air & Space Museum
Independence Avenue at 6th Street, SW
Washington, D.C. 20560
www.nasm.si.edu

The Smithsonian National Air and Space Museum (NASM) is located on the National Mall. The museum is wheelchair accessible. Visitors may borrow a wheelchair on a first-come, first-served basis at the security desk.

NASM displays space- and aviation-themed artifacts and exhibits. Visitors may also experience planetarium and IMAX shows or visit the astronomical observatory. There is no charge to visit the exhibits or observatory, but there is a fee to see an IMAX or planetarium show.

The observatory houses a 16-inch (41 cm) Boller and Chivens telescope, on loan from the Smithsonian's Oak Ridge Observatory in Massachusetts. The observatory dome is wheelchair accessible, and an ARE-125 articulated eyepiece allows people to view the image from a seated position. Portable telescopes are also available.

Views from the telescope are often displayed on monitors inside the observatory dome. The museum is planning to expand the telescope views to monitors inside the museum.

The observatory is open Thursday through Sunday from 10 a.m. to 2 p.m., weather permitting, and sometimes in the evening. You should check the viewing schedule at the museum welcome desk or on the website.

The Einstein Planetarium at NASM offers headsets with multi-language translation and volume amplification for each show. Captions can also be displayed upon request.

FLORIDA

BCC Planetarium and Observatory
Cocoa, Florida

Features: mobility access (planetarium)

Brevard Community College

Brevard Community College Planetarium and
Observatory
1519 Clearlake Road
Cocoa, Florida 32922
www.brevardcc.edu/planet

Brevard Community College is home to a planetarium and observatory. Located in scenic Cocoa, Florida, the planetarium and observatory are open to the public on Wednesdays, Fridays, and Saturdays. Check the website for specific hours.

An exhibit area in Astronaut Memorial Hall includes astronomy images, a Foucault pendulum, meteorites, and scales that tell you how much you weigh on other planets.

The planetarium is wheelchair accessible. The 24-inch (61 cm) telescope in the observatory is not wheelchair accessible; however, portable telescopes are provided on an accessible area of the roof.

GEORGIA

Fernbank Planetarium and Observatory
Atlanta, Georgia

Features: mobility access
(planetarium and exhibits only)

Fernbank Science Center

Fernbank Science Center
156 Heaton Park Drive
Atlanta, Georgia 30307
www.fernbank.edu

The Fernbank Science Center is open Monday through Saturday. Along with family friendly exhibits, the facility offers planetarium shows and night sky viewing in the observatory. There is no charge to visit the exhibits or observatory. The planetarium and exhibits are wheelchair accessible.

The observatory houses a 36-inch (91 cm) Cassegrain reflector, the largest telescope in the southeastern United States. Weather permitting, the observatory is open on Thursday and Friday evenings. The observatory dome is not wheelchair accessible; however, portable telescopes are available at ground level.

HAWAII

Imiloa Astronomy Center of Hawaii
Hilo, Hawaii

Features: mobility access,
assistive listening access

Imiloa Astronomy Center of Hawaii

Imiloa Astronomy Center of Hawaii
600 Imiloa Place
Hilo, Hawaii 96720
www.imiloahawaii.org

The Imiloa Astronomy Center of Hawaii is located on the campus of the University of Hilo, on the Big Island of Hawaii. The Astronomy Center is wheelchair accessible and includes exhibits, a planetarium, and a native garden. The exhibition area is divided into two major areas: Origins (of the cosmos and Earth) and Explorations (achievements of the Hawaiian exploration).

The planetarium presents an immersive experience, including 3-D programs. Assistive listening devices are available in the planetarium. Check the website for current show schedule and days of operation.

IDAHO

The Centennial Observatory
College of Southern Idaho
Twin Falls, Idaho

Features: mobility access, low vision access, assistive listening access, ASL (by request)

Joey Heck, Centennial Observatory

The College of Southern Idaho
315 Falls Avenue
Twin Falls, Idaho 83301
http://herrett.csi.edu

The Herrett Center for Arts & Science houses natural history and art galleries, the Faulkner

Planetarium, and the Centennial Observatory. The facility is located at the College of Southern Idaho and is open Tuesday through Saturday.

The Centennial Observatory opened to the public in 2004. A wheelchair lift brings visitors from the lobby to the observatory platform. The dome houses a 24-inch (61 cm) Ritchey-Chrétien telescope. Visitors view objects through the accessible ARE-125 eyepiece.

Video cameras attached to smaller telescopes, mounted on the main 24-inch telescope, broadcast live views from the telescope to the observatory lobby and locations throughout the museum. Portable telescopes are also available.

The planetarium has an assistive listening system. Sign language interpretation is available upon request.

A copy of the tactile astronomy book, **Touch the Universe**, is available for examination in the non-lending museum library.

ILLINOIS

Adler Planetarium
Chicago, Illinois

Features: mobility access, ASL (by request)

Craig Stillwell

The Adler Planetarium
1300 South Lake Shore Drive
Chicago, Illinois 60605
www.adlerplanetarium.org

The Adler Planetarium was founded in 1930 and is the oldest planetarium in the United States. It is located at the end of Lake Shore Drive in a scenic part of Chicago.

The Adler Planetarium is actually an astronomy learning center that features interactive space-related exhibits and two planetarium theaters. A limited number of wheelchairs are available for visitor use on a first-come, first-served basis.

The exhibition area and the Grainger and Definiti planetarium theaters are wheelchair accessible.

All of the chairs in the Grainger Sky Theater are removable, so there is no limit on wheelchair seating capacity.

The Definiti Theater is a steep, unidirectional theater with fixed seating. This theater can accommodate six wheelchairs per show. An additional six wheelchairs can be accommodated, but the staff needs 24 hours notice to remove some of the fixed seats.

Copies of most show scripts are available, and a special light can be set up for visitors who arrive with their own sign-language interpreters. Sign language interpretation can be provided by the Adler Planetarium but must be requested at least one week in advance of your visit.

INDIANA

Prairie Grass Observatory
North Frankfort, Indiana

Features: mobility access

Prairie Grass Observatory

Camp Cullom
Prairie Grass Observatory
6815 West County Road 200 N
Frankfort, Indiana 46041
www.indianastars.us

The Prairie Grass Observatory has four small
observatory buildings. Each building offers a

different telescope. The observatory buildings are all located adjacent to each other on a grassy field.

Three of the observatory buildings are accessible. Slide shows and videos are presented in the accessible amphitheater.

IOWA

Star Theater
Des Moines, Iowa
Features: mobility access

Science Center of Iowa

Star Theater

Science Center of Iowa

401 W. Martin Luther King Jr. Parkway

Des Moines, Iowa 50309

www.sciowa.org

The Science Center of Iowa is wheelchair accessible, and a limited number of wheelchairs are available for visitor use on a first-come, first-served basis.

The Science Center is home to a very unusual planetarium called the Star Theater. There are no fixed seats in the planetarium. A few portable chairs are provided for people who would like to sit, but most people sit or lie on the floor. Approximately thirty wheelchairs can fit in the Star Theatre for each show.

Live and pre-recorded programs are presented in the Star Theater each day, but the experience doesn't end there. Between shows, visitors can create their own planetarium programs using a technology called Cosmic Jukebox. Visitors select video clips from Cosmic Jukebox and combine them into a mini-show. Then they watch the show they produced on the Star Theater dome, with visuals and surround sound.

KANSAS

Powell Observatory
Louisburg, Kansas

Features: mobility access (classroom building and some telescopes), low vision access, captioning (classroom presentations)

Astronomical Society of Kansas City

Powell Observatory
26500 Melrose Street
Louisburg, Kansas 66053
www.askc.org/powell.htm

The Powell Observatory is located in the Lewis-Young Park on the northwest edge of Louisburg. The facility is composed of three observatory buildings with two of these buildings open to the public. The large rectangular building has a classroom with an accessible entrance and separate men's and women's restrooms. The restrooms are not wheelchair accessible. The accessible parking area is across the road just north of the classroom building, and a compacted gravel path leads to the observatory buildings. Donations of $6 per adult and $4 for children under twelve are requested, with all collected amounts used solely to maintain the observatory.

Night sky presentations begin in the classroom with illustrated and captioned PowerPoint slides. Weather permitting, visitors are then invited to view celestial objects through a variety of telescopes staffed by members of the Astronomical Society of Kansas City. These amateur astronomers also provide detailed descriptions of the sky for participants with visual impairments. Laser guided night sky tours of the constellations and bright stars are also offered.

The Powell Observatory buildings feature a 30-inch (76 cm) telescope, a 16-inch (41 cm) telescope, and a 12.5-inch (32 cm) telescope. These three telescopes are not wheelchair accessible, but construction plans have been made to install an adjustable height telescope that can be viewed from a seated position. Members of the astronomical society also bring up to 20 portable telescopes to the observatory grounds on viewing nights, so there are many opportunities to check out the sky.

Presentations on astronomy topics are offered every Saturday, May through October, and also by reservation. Check the website for current presentation and observing schedule.

LOUISIANA

Highland Park Road Observatory
Baton Rouge, Louisiana

Features: mobility access, low vision access

Highland Park Rd. Observatory

Highland Road Park Observatory
13800 Highland Road
Baton Rouge, Louisiana 70810
www.bro.lsu.edu

The Highland Park Road Observatory is operated in cooperation with the Parks and Recreation Commission of the Parish of East Baton Rouge (BREC), Louisiana State University (LSU) and the Baton Rouge Astronomical Society. BREC owns the observatory and land and provides an array of programs and activities; LSU owns the major equipment, and the Astronomical Society provides some equipment and the staff.

There are a 20-inch (51 cm) telescope, a 16-inch (41 cm) telescope, and several portable telescopes on the property. The main building houses the 20-inch telescope. The building itself is wheelchair accessible, but the 20-inch telescope is not. A live video feed from the 20 inch telescope can be broadcast onto a screen in the main building.

The 16-inch telescope, in the adjacent building, is wheelchair accessible and has an ARE-125 articulated eyepiece, which allows visitors in wheelchairs to view directly through the telescope. Viewing of the night sky with the 16-inch telescope is on Saturdays, by appointment.

Wheelchair accessible restrooms are available.

Astronomy and science lectures are presented on Friday evenings followed by observing. Saturday night observing does not include a lecture but sometimes does feature a physical science demonstration. All telescope observing is subject to weather conditions. Check the website for more information.

Irene Pennington Planetarium
Baton Rouge, Louisiana

Features: mobility access

Louisiana Art and Science Museum

Irene Pennington Planetarium
Louisiana Art and Science Museum
100 River Road South
Baton Rouge, Louisiana 70802
www.lasm.org

The Irene Pennington Planetarium is located
within the Louisiana Art and Science Museum,

along the bank of the Mississippi River in downtown Baton Rouge. This museum is unusual in that it combines the disciplines of art and science. As you enter the building, you turn left for science or right for the art gallery.

The exhibits in the Louisiana Art and Science Museum are organized in six themes: Ancient Egypt, Discovery Depot, Science Station, Solar System Gallery, Planet Tower and Universe Gallery. The Discovery Depot and Science Station areas offer many hands-on opportunities for young visitors to explore. The Solar System Gallery and Universe Gallery present exhibits on a variety of astronomical topics. Wondering how the planets in our solar system compare in size? Just look up for a scaled model of the planets suspended in the Planet Tower.

The museum and Pennington Planetarium are open Tuesday through Sunday; both are wheelchair accessible. Six wheelchairs can be accommodated in each planetarium show.

Public planetarium shows are presented several times a day. Visual rock music shows are presented on Friday evenings. Check the museum website for the current show schedule.

MAINE

Maynard F. Jordan Planetarium
Orono, Maine

Features: mobility access, tactile materials

Maynard F. Jordan Planetarium

Maynard F. Jordan Planetarium
5781 Wingate Hall
University of Maine
Orono, Maine 04469
www.GalaxyMaine.com

The Maynard F. Jordan Planetarium is the oldest planetarium in Maine. The planetarium is located on the second floor of Wingate Hall, on the campus of the University of Maine at Orono. Public planetarium shows are offered weekly though the school year and occasionally in the summer. All programs are about one hour long; check the planetarium website for the current show schedule.

The planetarium is wheelchair accessible. Three wheelchairs can be accommodated for each show.

Tactile materials are available in the planetarium lobby and include a touchable star chart, moon map, and map of the solar system.

The University also offers stargazing at the Maynard Jordan Observatory, located in a building near Smith Hall and the Memorial Union. The observatory building is not wheelchair accessible, but portable telescopes are available for use on the lawn outside. For the current observatory schedule, call the observatory hotline at (207) 581–1348.

USM Southworth Planetarium
Portland, Maine

Features: mobility access, ASL (by advance request)

Southworth Planetarium

Southworth Planetarium
University of Southern Maine
70 Falmouth Street
Portland, Maine 04103
www.usm.maine.edu/planet

The Southworth Planetarium is located in the Science Building on the University of Southern Maine's Portland campus.

The Science Building and Southworth Planetarium are wheelchair accessible. Four wheelchairs can comfortably fit in each planetarium show.

Public planetarium shows are generally presented on Friday evenings and on weekend afternoons.

Sign language interpretation is available but must be requested two weeks in advance through the planetarium website.

Telescopic viewing is offered on the last Wednesday of most months. A public science lecture series is presented on the third Thursday of each month.

Check the planetarium website for the current show schedule including specific dates for telescopic viewing and special lectures.

MARYLAND

Davis Planetarium
Baltimore, Maryland

Features: mobility access, low vision access, tactile exhibit materials

Maryland Science Center

Davis Planetarium
Maryland Science Center
601 Light Street
Baltimore, Maryland 21230
www.mdsci.org/planetarium/index.html

The Maryland Science Center is located on the scenic inner harbor in Baltimore. Three wheelchairs are available for visitor use on a first-come, first-served basis. Inquire at the ticket counter.

The St. John Properties IMAX Theater and the Davis Planetarium are both housed in the museum.

Astronomy programs are presented in the Davis Planetarium. This theater can fit up to four wheelchairs per show.

Although sign-language interpretation is not provided by the museum, planetarium staff can set up a special light for an interpreter who accompanies a visitor or group to a planetarium show.

Weather permitting, museum staff invite visitors to the rooftop observatory to safely view the Sun on Saturdays ("Sungazing Saturdays") and to stargaze on Friday evenings. The observatory is not wheelchair accessible; however, images from the observatory can be broadcast live to the planetarium and to the SpaceLink monitor on the second floor of the Science Center. Upon request, portable telescopes can be set up on the wheelchair accessible lower roof area, near the main observatory.

A new permanent astronomy exhibition, Life Beyond Earth, was scheduled to open in late 2012. The exhibit is a collaboration between Maryland Science Center staff and the Maryland School for the Blind. Several tactile components include models of the Milky Way galaxy, several extremophile microbes, and three tactile planetary surfaces. Braille booklets are available to accompany this exhibition.

MASSACHUSETTS

Clay Center Observatory
at Dexter and Southfield Schools
Brookline, Massachusetts
Features: mobility access, low vision access

Clay Center Observatory at Dexter and Southfield Schools

Clay Center Observatory
at Dexter and Southfield Schools
20 Newton Street
Brookline, Massachusetts 02445
www.claycenter.org
and www.clayobservatory.org

The Clay Center Observatory is located on the campus of the Dexter and Southfield Schools in Brookline, Massachusetts. The observatory is equipped with a custom-made, diffraction-limited, 25-inch (63 cm) f/9.6 Ritchey-Chrétien reflecting telescope, similar in optical design to the Hubble Space Telescope. The telescope is fully automated and can be operated remotely from any computer in the world via the Internet.

The observatory is wheelchair accessible, and an ARE-125 articulated eyepiece makes viewing through the telescope possible for anyone in a wheelchair. Portable telescopes are usually available on the accessible roof deck during open nights. Check the Clay Center website in advance for the schedule of public open nights, for weather reports, and to register in advance with any request for accessibility or assistance. Questions may be asked on the registration form or by calling the Clay Center information line posted on the website.

A live video feed from the telescope can be viewed from a monitor in the dome or streamed to other locations on campus or to the Internet.

The Clay Center has some auditory exhibits in the multi-purpose room adjacent to the observatory. These resources include meteorites, a copy of the tactile astronomy book **Touch the Sun**, a 3-D solar system model, a talking solar system information and quiz console, and live astronomer tour guides.

Alden Digital Planetarium
Worcester, Massachusetts

Features: mobility access

Ecotarium

Alden Digital Planetarium

Ecotarium

222 Harrington Way

Worcester, Massachusetts 01604

www.ecotarium.org/planetarium

The Ecotarium is a place to explore and connect with science and nature. Located in Worcester, Massachusetts, this science center combines indoor programs and exhibits with outdoor nature trails, wildlife, and even a narrow-gauge railroad. Two wheelchairs can be accommodated on each train ride.

The museum building features three floors of participatory exhibits relating to science and New England ecology.

The Ecotarium is open Tuesdays through Sundays, and the museum building is wheelchair accessible.

The Alden Digital Planetarium, located in the museum building, was the first digital planetarium in Massachusetts. The planetarium features daily programs for family-friendly audiences.

Six visitors in wheelchairs can be accommodated during each planetarium show.

MICHIGAN

Delta College Planetarium
and Learning Center
Bay City, Michigan
Features: mobility access

Delta College Planetarium and Learning Center

Delta College Planetarium and Learning Center
100 Center Avenue
Bay City, Michigan 48708
www.delta.edu/planet

The Delta College Planetarium and Learning Center presents programs for the general public and is used in astronomy courses at Delta College. Public shows are scheduled Tuesday through Thursday and Saturday through Sunday.

The planetarium is wheelchair accessible, and six wheelchairs can be accommodated in each show. Some planetarium shows are interactive; the audience participates by pressing buttons on their seats. Special interactive controls are also available for visitors in wheelchairs.

When the facility offers evening stargazing, portable telescopes are set up on the observation deck.

Check the website for show and event schedules.

Calvin Observatory
Grand Rapids, Michigan

Features: mobility access (restricted),
low vision access

Larry Molnar, Calvin Observatory

Calvin College Observatory
Calvin College
North Hall
3201 Burton SE
Grand Rapids, MI 49546
www.calvin.edu/academic/phys/observatory

The Calvin Observatory is located at Calvin College in Grand Rapids, Michigan. The entrance is at the North Hall Building.

Public open nights are held at the Calvin Observatory on clear Wednesday evenings throughout the year. The observatory dome housing the 16-inch (41 cm) telescope is not wheelchair accessible. However, with advance notice, the observatory staff can set up portable 8-inch (20 cm) telescopes in an accessible area.

Visitors who are not restricted by mobility access can watch the enlarged view from the telescope, projected on a monitor inside the observatory dome.

MINNESOTA

Onan Observatory
Norwood–Young America, Minnesota
Features: mobility access, low vision access

Merle Hiltner, Minnesota Astronomical Society

Onan Observatory
10775 County Road 33
Norwood–Young America, Minnesota 55397
www.mnastro.org/onan

Onan Observatory is located within the Carver County–Baylor regional park. The Minnesota Astronomical Society presents regularly scheduled public star parties at the Onan Observatory. The observatory building, which houses a 16-inch (41 cm) and two 14-inch (36 cm) Schmidt-Cassegrain telescopes, is wheelchair accessible. Several monitors show live views of objects from cameras mounted to the telescope. Portable telescopes, including a 20-inch (51 cm) Dobsonian, are also often available.

The star parties are popular, with 50 to 300 people in attendance.

MISSOURI

Arvin Gottlieb Planetarium
Kansas City, Missouri
Features: mobility access

Matt Christopher

Arvin Gottlieb Planetarium
Science City at Union Station
30 W. Pershing Road
Kansas City, Missouri 64108
www.sciencecity.com/planetarium.html

Union Station was built in 1914 and used as a busy train station until the 1980s. The 850,000 square foot facility was then closed and transformed into a complex of restaurants, shops, a science center, and an Amtrak train stop.

Science City is home to interactive science exhibits, activities, a large format theater, and the Arvin Gottlieb Planetarium. A limited number of wheelchairs are available for visitors on a first-come, first-served basis at the entrance to the science center.

The planetarium is wheelchair accessible and can accommodate twelve wheelchairs in each show. Planetarium shows are presented Tuesdays through Sundays.

Saint Louis Science Center
St. Louis, Missouri
Features: mobility access,
assistive listening access

Saint Louis Science Center

Saint Louis Science Center
5050 Oakland Avenue
Saint Louis, Missouri 63110
www.slsc.org

The James McDonnell Planetarium is located
within the Saint Louis Science Center. This is a

unique planetarium, because the theater does not have fixed seating. There are only a few portable chairs, as well as some mats, in case visitors would like to lie down while learning about astronomy. The planetarium could fit about 300 fixed seats but instead is known as the most wheelchair accessible planetarium in the country.

The planetarium also has a limited number of assistive listening devices available.

Weather permitting, free public telescope viewing is offered on the first Friday of every month beginning at 7 p.m. (8 p.m. during summer months) from January through December, with members of the St. Louis Astronomical Society assisting. Portable telescopes are set up on the Archery field adjacent to the Planetarium parking lot.

MONTANA

Taylor Planetarium
Bozeman, Montana
Features: mobility access

Museum of the Rockies

Taylor Planetarium
Museum of the Rockies
600 W. Kagy Boulevard
Bozeman, Montana 59717
http://www.museumoftherockies.org/exhibits

The Taylor Planetarium is located within the Museum of the Rockies. The museum is open daily. Pre-recorded planetarium shows are presented each day, and live tours of the night sky are presented on weekends. Check the web page for current show schedule.

A limited number of wheelchairs are available for visitor use, on a first-come, first-served basis, at the front desk.

The Taylor Planetarium is wheelchair accessible. Eight wheelchairs can be accommodated in each planetarium show.

The Destination Space exhibit area features space-related exhibits and artifacts. Young visitors will enjoy the Kid Space exhibit area that features brightly colored signage and hands-on activities.

NEBRASKA

J.M. McDonald Planetarium
Hastings, Nebraska
Features: mobility access

Hastings Museum

J.M. McDonald Planetarium

Hastings Museum

1330 N. Burlington Ave.

Hastings, Nebraska 68901

Hastingsmuseum.org/planetarium/current-shows

The Hastings Natural and Cultural History Museum is open daily in the summer and closed on Mondays during the school year. Pre-recorded full dome programs are presented six days a week, and current sky shows are presented five days a week.

The McDonald Planetarium is wheelchair accessible and can house three wheelchairs per show.

The museum offers safe viewing of the Sun, weather permitting, on the first Saturday of each month, from 11 a.m. to noon. Check the solar viewing web page for the current schedule, at http://hastingsmuseum.org/planetarium /solar-observing-free.

Ralph Mueller Planetarium
Lincoln, Nebraska

Features: mobility access

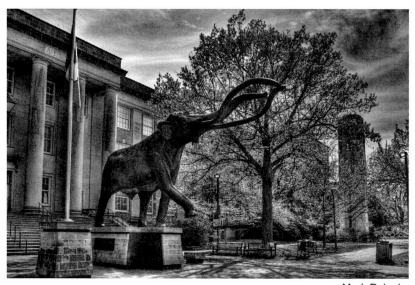

Mark Dahmke

Ralph Mueller Planetarium
University of Nebraska State Museum
14th and U Streets
Morrill Hall
Lincoln, Nebraska 68588
www.spacelaser.com

The Ralph Mueller Planetarium is located in Morrill Hall on the campus of the University of Nebraska–Lincoln. The museum has two wheelchairs available for visitor use.

The planetarium is wheelchair accessible. Three wheelchairs can comfortably fit inside, with a maximum of eleven wheelchairs per show.

Public planetarium programs are presented on weekends during the school year and on Tuesday through Sunday during the summer. Check the planetarium website for the current show schedule.

NEVADA

Jack C. Davis Observatory
Carson City, Nevada

Features: mobility access, low vision access

Robert Collier, Jack C. Davis Observatory

Jack C. Davis Observatory
Western Nevada College
2699 Van Patten Drive
Carson City, Nevada 89703
www.wnc.edu/observatory

The Western Nevada Astronomical Society presents public viewing each Saturday evening at the Jack C. Davis Observatory. On the first

Saturday of each month, the observatory hosts a telescope clinic where visitors are invited to bring their own telescope to use. Astronomical society members can also assist with slight telescope repairs and provide instruction on how to use a telescope.

On remaining Saturday evenings, an astronomy lecture is presented before viewing in the Jack C. Davis Observatory. Additional observing is scheduled during astronomical events such as eclipses and meteor showers. Sky viewing is weather dependent, and it's a good idea to check the website for updates to the viewing schedule.

The 2,800 square foot facility houses 16-inch (41 cm), 14-inch (36 cm), and 10-inch (25 cm) telescopes. Accessible parking and sidewalks provide access to the observatory. The restrooms are accessible. The observatory building is wheelchair accessible; but, depending on the sky angle of the object being viewed, the telescopes may not be. However, the views from the telescopes are usually visible on computer screens in the telescope room.

College of Southern Nevada Planetarium
North Las Vegas, Nevada

Features: mobility access, low vision access,
ASL (by advance request)

Dale Etheridge

The College of Southern Nevada (CSN)
Planetarium
3200 E. Cheyenne Avenue
North Las Vegas, Nevada 89030
www.csn.edu/planetarium

The planetarium at the College of Southern
Nevada offers public planetarium shows
on Friday evenings and Saturday afternoon
and evenings. The planetarium is wheelchair
accessible; six wheelchairs can fit in each show.

Visitors may request a sign language interpreter
but must provide several days notice by sending
an email message to the planetarium director at
planetarium@csn.edu.

Weather permitting, after the 7:30 pm
planetarium shows on Friday and Saturday,
visitors are invited to view sky objects in
the student observatory. The observatory
is wheelchair accessible, and a video camera
can be installed to project the image from
the eyepiece to a monitor. Check the CSN
planetarium website for the current planetarium
and observatory schedule.

NEW HAMPSHIRE

McAuliffe-Shepard Discovery Center, Concord, New Hampshire

Features: mobility access, assistive listening access, ASL (Aerospacefest only)

McAuliffe-Shepard Discovery Center

McAuliffe-Shepard Discovery Center
2 Institute Drive
Concord, New Hampshire 03301
www.starhop.com

The McAuliffe-Shepard Discovery Center is dedicated to two New Hampshire space pioneers, NASA Teacher-in-Space Christa McAuliffe and America's first astronaut, Alan Shepard. The Discovery Center houses interactive exhibits, a planetarium, an observatory, a science store, and a cafe.

A wheelchair and motorized scooter are available for use by visitors on a first-come, first served basis. The planetarium theater is wheelchair accessible and six wheelchairs can be accommodated in each show.

An assistive listening system is available for planetarium shows. A magnetic loop enabling visitors with telecoil-equipped hearing aids to hear the program narration with full clarity is also available in the planetarium.

The two floors of galleries and exhibits are wheelchair accessible via a glass elevator.

The observatory is not wheelchair accessible; however, portable telescopes are set up on the first Friday of each month, weather permitting, and at other times if requested for reasons of accessibility.

The McAuliffe-Shepard Discovery Center presents an annual Aerospacefest on the first Friday night and Saturday in May. As part of this celebration, mainstage programs are signed by ASL interpreters.

NEW JERSEY

Edelman Planetarium
Glassboro, New Jersey
Features: mobility access

Edelman Planetarium

Edelman Planetarium
Rowan University
201 Mullica Hill Road
Glassboro, New Jersey 08028
www.rowan.edu/planetarium

The Edelman Planetarium is located on the campus of Rowan University in the Science Hall. The Science Hall is located on the north side of Route 322 between Savitz Hall and Westby Hall and across from Robinson Hall on Meditation Walk.

The planetarium is wheelchair accessible; up to eight wheelchairs can fit in each show.

Public planetarium shows are presented once a week, on Sunday afternoons, during the school year. Programs for school groups are presented by reservation. Groups with more then two wheelchairs should provide advance notice to the planetarium director. Check the website for current show schedule.

William D. McDowell Observatory
Lyndhurst, New Jersey

Features: mobility access, low vision access, tactile materials, assistive listening access, captioning

Photo Courtesy of NJ Meadowlands Commission

William D. McDowell Observatory
Three Dekorte Park Plaza
Lyndhurst, New Jersey 07071
www.rst2.edu/meadowlands/observatory

The McDowell Observatory is part of the Meadowlands Environment Center, a New Jersey Meadowlands Commission facility operated by Ramapo College of New Jersey. The Observatory is open to the public on Monday and Wednesday evenings, weather permitting.

The dome is wheelchair accessible, but viewing through the telescope requires climbing 25 steps. The image from the telescope can be seen from a monitor in the dome and in a classroom. Portable telescopes are available by request.

Current sky information is available on site in Braille, and tactile materials are available. The staff describes telescopic objects very clearly.

Assistive listening devices are available. The staff person wears a microphone, and the visitor listens on a volume-adjustable headset.

The image from the telescope, as seen on the monitor, is captioned.

Dreyfuss Planetarium
Newark, New Jersey

Features: mobility access, assistive listening access

Newark Museum in Newark's Downtown/Arts District

Dreyfuss Planetarium

Newark Museum

49 Washington Street

Newark, New Jersey 07102

www.newarkmuseum.org

New Jersey's first planetarium, the Alice and Leonard Dreyfuss Planetarium, is located in the Newark Museum, in Newark's downtown Arts District. The museum and planetarium are both wheelchair accessible. Up to four wheelchairs can be accommodated for each planetarium show. Of the fixed seats in the planetarium, four seats are available as transfer seats with hinged armrests.

An assistive listening system is available in the planetarium.

Public planetarium shows are generally presented on Wednesday through Sunday afternoons. It is best to check the website for the current show schedule.

Planetarium staff occasionally set up portable telescopes for stargazing. The observing schedule is posted on the home page.

RVCC Reeve Planetarium
North Branch, New Jersey

Features: mobility access, tactile materials, programs for visitors on the autism spectrum

Raritan Valley Community College

Reeve Planetarium
Raritan Valley Community College
1170 Route 28
North Branch, New Jersey 08876
www.raritanval.edu/planetarium

An interview with the planetarium director begins on page 48.

The Reeve Planetarium is located on the campus of Raritan Valley Community College. A variety of planetarium shows (including special shows for visitors on the autism spectrum), laser shows, and concerts are held in the planetarium. Public programs are offered on Saturdays and some Sundays from October through May. Daily programs are offered on school holidays and during the summer. Check the website for the current schedule.

The planetarium is wheelchair accessible; eight wheelchairs can be accommodated in each show.

Tactile resources include meteorite samples, a space shuttle model, and copies of the Braille book, **Touch the Stars**.

Visitors are welcome to view the night sky at the accessible RVCC observatory. An ARE-125 articulated relay eyepiece allows visitors in wheelchairs to view directly through the telescope eyepiece.

New Jersey State Museum Planetarium
Trenton, New Jersey

Features: mobility access, assistive listening access, ASL (by advance request)

New Jersey State Museum

New Jersey State Museum Planetarium
New Jersey State Museum
205 West State Street
Trenton, New Jersey 08625
www.newjerseystatemuseum.org

The New Jersey State Museum is home to the New Jersey State Museum Planetarium. The museum and planetarium are open Tuesday through Saturday, and both are wheelchair accessible.

Five wheelchairs can be accommodated in each planetarium show.

An assistive listening system is available for planetarium shows. Sign language interpretation is available but must be requested from the museum two weeks in advance of visit.

The New Jersey State Museum Planetarium offers a variety of planetarium shows each day. Some shows are geared toward young children, while other shows are for the general public. Check the home page for the current planetarium show schedule.

NEW MEXICO

Robert H. Goddard Planetarium
Roswell, New Mexico
Features: mobility access

Roswell Museum and Art Center

Robert H. Goddard Planetarium
100 W. 11th Street
Roswell, New Mexico 88201
www.roswellmuseum.org

The Robert H. Goddard Planetarium is a joint venture between the Roswell Independent School District and the city of Roswell. Primarily providing services to schools, the planetarium also provides programs and services to the community and southeastern New Mexico.

The planetarium is wheelchair accessible; six wheelchairs can fit comfortably inside the theater for each show. Some tactile materials are also available.

Science and space camps are held for children through grade six during the summer. Each year the planetarium participates in the annual Roswell UFO Festival, during the week of July 4th, with planetarium shows, laser shows, and children's activities. Monthly Science Saturday programs for children and adults are presented during the year. Check the website for the current schedule.

National Radio Astronomy Observatory
Very Large Array
Socorro, New Mexico

Features: mobility access (visitor center)

Image courtesy of NRAO/AUI (www.nrao.edu)
and Kristal Armendariz, photographer

NRAO Very Large Array
Array Operations Center
P.O. Box O
1003 Lopezville Road
Socorro, New Mexico 87801
www.vla.nrao.edu

The Very Large Array (VLA) is located at 7,000 feet (2,100 m) elevation and 50 miles (80 km) west of Socorro. Take Highway 60 to mile marker 93. The turnoff road is rural road 52, and the VLA is 4 miles (6 km) from the highway turnoff.

The visitor center is wheelchair accessible and is open every day until dusk. Guests may follow a one-quarter-mile, level, self-guided tour of the facility. Special guided tours are offered on certain dates. Check the home page for more information.

The VLA is home to 27 independent radio telescopes that are positioned in a Y-shaped pattern. Each radio telescope is 82 feet (25 m) in diameter; the array has the resolution of a single radio telescope 22 miles (36 km) across.

The radio telescopes are very sensitive to interference, so cell phones may not be used.

NEW YORK

Columbia University
Astronomy Outreach
New York, New York
Features: mobility access (limited)

Columbia University

Columbia University Astronomy Outreach

Columbia University

Pupin Physics Laboratory

550 West 120th Street

New York, New York 10027

outreach.astro.columbia.edu

The Columbia University Astronomy Outreach Department offers astronomy programs every other Friday and includes a lecture and stargazing. The 30-minute lecture is held in a fully wheelchair accessible lecture hall. The lectures may also include supplemental slide shows, 3-D visualizations, and discussions. Expect between 100 and 250 to attend these popular talks.

Weather permitting, the staff invites visitors to the rooftop observatory for 90 minutes of stargazing. The observatory is not wheelchair accessible; however, portable telescopes are sometimes available at ground level. It is best to check in advance. The university does not have designated parking. All parking is on nearby streets or in nearby private garages.

A separate Sidewalk Astronomy program is also offered. Once a month, staff brings portable telescopes into Harlem at the corner of 125th Street and Adam Clayton Powell Boulevard. Check the website for schedules on the

Sidewalk Astronomy program and on-campus astronomy events for the public.

The website also has information on how to join the Columbia University Astronomy Outreach Facebook page.

Rose Center for Earth and Space
New York, New York

Features: mobility access,
assistive listening access

Denis Finnin ©American Museum of Natural History

Rose Center for Earth and Space
American Museum of Natural History
Central Park West at 79th Street
New York, New York 10024
www.amnh.org/rose

The Rose Center for Earth and Space Science is part of the American Museum of Natural History. All of the museum exhibits and theaters, including the Hayden Planetarium, are wheelchair accessible.

An audio tour, via a wand or headset listening device, is available free with museum admission or membership. This 75-minute tour, available in English or Spanish, guides visitors through a variety of Earth and Space exhibits in the Rose Center.

An assistive listening system is available in the Hayden Planetarium, by request, for volume amplification.

Open captioning is not available in the planetarium but is provided in most exhibit theaters throughout the museum. Transcripts of planetarium shows can be downloaded from the museum website.

NORTH CAROLINA

Pisgah Astronomical Research Institute
Rosman, North Carolina

Features: mobility access, tactile materials

PARI

Pisgah Astronomical Research Institute
1 PARI Drive
Rosman, North Carolina 28772
www.pari.edu

The Pisgah Astronomical Research Institute (PARI) is a research, education, and public science center in western North Carolina. The 200-acre campus houses radio and optical telescopes. All of the buildings on the main campus are wheelchair accessible. The radio telescopes and many of the optical telescopes are operated from a control room in the administration building.

Public sessions are held in the evening once a month and during special astronomical events. Portable telescopes are available.

Tactile materials about the Moon are available.

OHIO

Cincinnati Observatory
Cincinnati, Ohio
Features: mobility access

Cincinnati Observatory

Cincinnati Observatory
3489 Observatory Place
Cincinnati, Ohio 45208
www.cincinnatiobservatory.org

The Cincinnati Observatory sits atop
Mt. Lookout in Cincinnati and is designated as
a National Historic Landmark. The observatory

has two telescopes, housed in two different buildings. The 11-inch (28 cm) Merz and Mahler telescope and the 16-inch (41 cm) Alvan Clark refractor telescope are used in public education programs.

The exhibits and classroom interior floors in both observatory buildings are wheelchair accessible; however, the telescope domes are not accessible. Staff is able to provide portable telescopes for viewing outside.

Check with the observatory staff for public observing dates.

Caryl D. Philips Space Theater
Dayton, Ohio

Features: mobility access, tactile materials

Boonshoft Museum of Discovery

Caryl D. Philips Space Theater

Boonshoft Museum of Discovery

2600 DeWeese Parkway

Dayton, Ohio 45414

www.Boonshoftmuseum.org

The Caryl D. Philips Space Theater is located in the Boonshoft Museum of Discovery. The

Boonshoft Museum is open daily but closed on major holidays. Check the museum web page for the operating schedule.

The museum and the space theater are wheelchair accessible. A limited number of wheelchairs are available for visitor use on a first-come, first-served basis. Inquire at the front desk. Eight wheelchairs can be accommodated in each planetarium show.

The space theater offers a minimum of one live planetarium show, one full dome astronomy show, and one 3D show each day. Full dome shows are family-friendly films that feature an astronomy theme.

Special presentations called Evenings of Astronomy are offered the third Friday of each month. These programs cover specific astronomy topics of interest, such as how to use a telescope, what light pollution is, and the life of a star. For current schedule of programs, check the space theater schedule, on the museum web page.

The Hall of the Universe exhibition features exhibits with visual, auditory, and tactile components. Additional tactile components are available but must be requested in advance. Contact the astronomy department at astronomy@boonshoftmuseum.org before your visit to ensure astronomy tactile materials will be available on the day of your visit.

The Apollo Observatory is not wheelchair accessible. However, a 2013 astronomy exhibit renovation is scheduled to include a new live feed link from the telescope to an accessible location in the museum.

Ward Beecher Planetarium
Youngstown, Ohio

Features: mobility access, tactile materials

Youngstown State University

Ward Beecher Planetarium

Youngstown State University

Ward Beecher Science Hall, Room 2001

Youngstown, Ohio 44555

www.wbplanetarium.org

The Ward Beecher Planetarium is located on the campus of Youngstown State University. The planetarium was named after local philanthropist Ward Beecher, whose donation paid for an expansion of the university science building and construction of the planetarium. The planetarium opened in 1966 and has been used as a school and community resource. The equipment underwent a major upgrade in 2006.

The Ward Beecher Planetarium is located in room 2001 of the Ward Beecher Science Hall. The planetarium is wheelchair accessible; three wheelchairs can be comfortably accommodated in each show.

There is a small parking lot near the science building with four handicapped parking spot. However, Youngstown State University requires that anyone parking in those spots have both a YSU parking permit and an official state permit. It is recommended that drivers with passengers needing mobility access drop off their passengers and then re-park in a nearby lot.

Public planetarium shows are presented during the school year on Friday evenings and Saturday afternoons and evenings.

Planetarium staff occasionally set-up portable telescopes on the nearby sidewalk for stargazing.

Tactile materials, including a copy of **Touch the Stars**, are available for use in the planetarium.

OKLAHOMA

Kirkpatrick Planetarium
Oklahoma City, Oklahoma

Features: mobility access,
ASL (by advance request)

Science Museum Oklahoma

Kirkpatrick Planetarium
Science Museum Oklahoma
2100 NE 52nd Street
Oklahoma City, Oklahoma 73132
www.sciencemuseumok.org/planetarium.html

The Kirkpatrick Planetarium is located within Science Museum Oklahoma. The museum and planetarium are open daily. Several planetarium show are presented daily. The museum also houses an IMAX theater, called the Domed Theater, that presents large screen films.

Wheelchairs are available for loan on a first-come, first-served basis, at the front desk. The Kirkpatrick Planetarium is wheelchair accessible; five wheelchairs can be accommodated during each show.

ASL interpretation is available but must be requested several days in advance.

Directional lighting is available for any sign-language interpreter who is accompanying visitors in the planetarium.

OREGON

Kendall Planetarium
Portland, Oregon
Features: mobility access,
assistive listening access

Oregon Museum of Science and Industry

Kendall Planetarium
Oregon Museum of Science and Industry
1945 SE Water Avenue
Portland, Oregon 97214
www.omsi.edu/planetarium

The Kendall Planetarium is located within the Oregon Museum of Science and Industry (OMSI). The Museum is open every day. A limited number of wheelchairs are available for visitor use on a first-come, first-served basis. Request a wheelchair to the right of the ticket booth.

All exhibit and lab areas are wheelchair accessible with the exception of the U.S.S. Blueback submarine.

While all exhibits and labs are visual, many of these areas have additional auditory or tactile components that invite visitor participation.

The Kendall Planetarium offers several planetarium shows each day. On Friday and Saturday evenings, visitors can attend laser light shows. These programs combine vivid light designs with rock music. Laser light shows often include flashing images.

The planetarium is wheelchair accessible and can accommodate six to twelve wheelchairs in each show.

An assistive listening (telecoil loop) system allows visitors with compatible hearing aids to tap into the audio of the shows. Contact the planetarium to inquire if your hearing aid works with this system.

Copies of the planetarium show scripts are available upon request.

Sunriver Nature Center and Observatory
Sunriver, Oregon

Features: mobility access, low vision access

Sunriver Nature Center

Sunriver Nature Center and Observatory

57245 River Road

Sunriver, Oregon 97707

www.sunrivernaturecenter.org

The Sunriver Nature Center is home to interpretive exhibits, educational programs, a botanical garden, nature trails, and an observatory. The observatory is wheelchair accessible; on a busy night, 8 to 10 telescopes may be in operation. Images from the telescopes may also be viewed on a monitor.

The observatory is open over two hundred nights a year. Because the viewing schedule varies by season, it is best to check the website for the up-to-date observing schedule.

PENNSYLVANIA

North Museum Planetarium
Lancaster, Pennsylvania

Features: mobility access

North Museum of Natural History and Science

North Museum Planetarium
North Museum of Natural History and Science
400 College Avenue
Lancaster, Pennsylvania 17603
www.northmuseum.org/Planetarium

The North Museum is located near Franklin and Marshall College in Lancaster, Pennsylvania. The Museum is open Tuesday through Sunday and is wheelchair accessible through a ramp at the side of the building. A wheelchair is available for visitor use on a first-come, first-served basis.

The North Museum Planetarium opened in 1953 and has recently been upgraded to provide a more visually immersive experience. Pre-recorded and live planetarium shows are presented on weekends during the school year and Tuesday through Sunday, during the summer. Check the home page for current show schedule.

Four visitors with wheelchairs can be accommodated for each planetarium show.

Fels Planetarium
Philadelphia, Pennsylvania

Features: mobility access,
assistive listening access

Franklin Institute

Fels Planetarium
Franklin Institute
222 N. 20th Street
Philadelphia, Pennsylvania 19103
www2.fi.edu/theater/planetarium
/theater-info.php

The Fels Planetarium is located in the historic Franklin Institute in Philadelphia. The Franklin Institute is closed on Thanksgiving, Christmas Day, and the annual Franklin Awards Day in April. Check the website for current schedule and any closures.

The museum is wheelchair accessible, and a limited number of wheelchairs are available on a first-come, first-served basis at the Atrium Information Desk or at the 20th Street Business Desk.

Ten wheelchairs can be accommodated in each planetarium show.

Assistive listening devices are available to use in the Fels Planetarium, the Tuttleman IMAX Theater, and the auditorium and demonstration theaters. A limited number of assistive listening devices are available at the box office.

The planetarium offers a mixed schedule of pre-recorded full-dome shows on various topics and live sky shows, guiding audiences on a tour through the night sky. Some of the planetarium shows have flashing lights and fast motion. If this is a concern, it is best to contact the Fels Planetarium with specific questions.

The Fels Planetarium hosts monthly meetings of the local Rittenhouse Astronomical Society.

SOUTH CAROLINA

DuPont Planetarium
Aiken, South Carolina

Features: mobility access, low vision access, assistive listening access

University of South Carolina

DuPont Planetarium
Ruth Patrick Science Education Center
University of South Carolina–Aiken
471 University Parkway
Aiken, South Carolina 29801
http://rpsec.usca.edu/planetarium

The Dupont Planetarium is located in the Ruth Patrick Science Education Center (RPSEC), on the campus of the University of South Carolina–Aiken. RPSEC is a cooperative effort by the University of South Carolina–Aiken, local industry, and public school districts in the central Savannah River area. During the academic year, the science center is used as a resource for local primary and secondary schools on weekdays.

RPSEC and the DuPont Planetarium are wheelchair accessible. Two wheelchairs can be accommodated in each planetarium show.

During the school year, public planetarium shows are presented on Saturdays. The public schedule changes to Tuesdays through Thursdays from June through August. Check the website for current show schedule.

An assistive listening system is available in the planetarium. The staff requests that you contact them 24 hours in advance to use an assistive listening headset.

The rooftop observatory at the science center is not wheelchair accessible. However, live images from the telescope can be transmitted to an accessible viewing location.

TENNESSEE

Sharpe Planetarium
Memphis, Tennessee

Features: mobility access,
assistive listening access

Pink Palace Museum

Sharpe Planetarium
Pink Palace Museum
3050 Central Avenue
Memphis, Tennessee, 38111
www.memphismuseums.org

The Sharpe Planetarium is located in the Pink Palace Museum. The museum is open every day except Thanksgiving Day, Christmas Day, and New Year's Day.

The Pink Palace Museum was originally planned as an estate for Clarence Saunders, founder of the Piggly Wiggly grocery chain. Saunders lost his fortune in the early 1920s and never had the opportunity to live in the mansion. The property was eventually donated to the city of Memphis and opened in 1930 as the Memphis Museum of Natural History and Industrial Arts. Several exhibits and a planetarium were added in the 1950s. The museum was renamed the Pink Palace Museum in 1967. A larger building was constructed next to the original mansion and opened in 1977.

The Pink Palace Museum is wheelchair accessible. Two wheelchairs are available for use in the museum on a first-come, first-served basis.

The Sharpe Planetarium is wheelchair accessible; six wheelchairs can fit in each show. Planetarium programs are presented on Tuesdays through Saturdays.

An assistive listening system is available for the planetarium. Request an assistive listening unit at the ticket booth.

TEXAS

Cook Education Center Planetarium
Corsicana, Texas
Features: mobility access

Cook Education Center Planetarium

Cook Education Center Planetarium
Navarro College
3100 West Collin St.
Corsicana, Texas 75110
www.cookplanetarium.us

The Cook Education Center planetarium is located on the campus of Navarro College. On weekdays, the planetarium is used exclusively for school groups and Navarro College courses. Public planetarium shows are generally scheduled on Saturday afternoons. The planetarium schedule is posted on the planetarium website and can also be accessed through the planetarium hotline at (903) 874–1211.

The Cook Planetarium has a sixty-foot diameter dome ceiling and seats 200 visitors. The theater is wheelchair accessible; six wheelchairs can comfortably fit inside per show.

Although the planetarium does not have sign language interpreters available on staff, they can turn on a special light to illuminate a visiting interpreter. Staff can also provide copies of the planetarium show scripts in advance.

McDonald Observatory
Mt. Locke, Texas

Features: mobility access

McDonald Observatory

McDonald Observatory
Frank N. Bash Visitors Center
3640 Dark Sky Drive
McDonald Observatory, Texas 79734
mcdonaldobservatory.org/visitors

The University of Texas at Austin's McDonald
Observatory is located in the Davis Mountains
of West Texas at about 6,500 feet (2,000 m)
elevation. The Frank N. Bash Visitors Center is
open most days except Thanksgiving, Christmas,

and New Year's Day. During the day, guests can participate in solar viewing, explore the exhibit hall, enjoy a presentation, or visit the research facilities on a self-guided tour. Weather permitting, evening sky viewing with telescopes at the visitor center is scheduled during several nights each week. The Wren-Marcario Accessible Telescope is designed to be 100 percent wheelchair accessible and is located at the visitor center. This telescope is described in detail on pages 5 and 6 of this book.

There is no fee to visit the McDonald Observatory and take a self-guided tour. Tickets for a guided tour (which includes access to the visitor center), star parties, and other organized programs may be purchased online through the McDonald Observatory home page. Because up to 60,000 people visit the McDonald Observatory each year, advance online purchase is recommended.

Center for Earth and Space Science Education Planetarium Tyler, Texas

Features: mobility access, tactile materials

Tyler Junior College

The Center for Earth and Space
Science Education
Tyler Junior College
1411 E. Lake Street
Tyler, Texas 75701
www.tjc.edu/cesse

The Center for Earth and Space Science Education (CESSE) is located on the campus of Tyler Junior College. The facility serves the East Texas community through programs, services, and collaborations.

CESSE offers visitors hands-on exhibits, including meteorite specimens, and large screen image displays from NASA and the Space Telescope Science Institute. The facility is wheelchair accessible; four visitors in wheelchairs can be accommodated for each planetarium show.

The CESSE planetarium presents a variety of programs for school groups and the general public including pre-recorded programs and the live show East Texas Skies. Other presentations have included classical music and rock music in the planetarium dome.

The CESSE planetarium has also been host to special lectures and science-related events. Check the home page for the current show and event schedule.

UTAH

Clark Planetarium
Salt Lake City, Utah
Features: mobility access,
assistive listening access (IMAX only)

Seth Jarvis

Clark Planetarium
110 South 400 West
Salt Lake City, Utah 84101
www.clarkplanetarium.org

The Clark Planetarium is open every day except
Thanksgiving, Christmas Eve, and Christmas

Day. It is conveniently located in downtown Salt Lake City and easily accessed via the TRAX light rail public transit system. The closest transit stop is the Planetarium TRAX station.

The Clark Planetarium houses 10,000 square feet of astronomy and space exploration exhibits plus the ATK IMAX Theatre and Hansen Dome Theatre. Planetarium shows are presented in the Hansen Dome Theatre.

Planetarium shows are designed as a 360-degree immersive visual experience using full dome technology. Each planetarium show can accommodate six wheelchairs.

An assistive listening system is available in the IMAX Theatre only.

VIRGINIA

John C. Wells Planetarium
Harrisonburg, Virginia

Features: mobility access, low vision access

James Madison University

John C. Wells Planetarium
James Madison University
91 E. Grace Street
Harrisonburg, Virginia 22807
www.jmu.edu/planetarium

The John C. Wells Planetarium is located in room 1103 in Miller Hall at James Madison University. The planetarium is located on the first floor and is wheelchair accessible. Two wheelchairs can be accommodated for each show.

Free planetarium shows are presented to the public every Saturday at 2:30 and 3:30 pm during the academic year. Shows include a pre-recorded planetarium program followed by a live tour of the beautiful Shenandoah Valley night sky.

Weather permitting, stargazing is presented on the last Friday of each month in Astronomy Park. Portable telescopes are set up in the meadow behind the Physics/Chemistry Building. A map with written travel directions to Astronomy Park is available at www.jmu.edu/planetarium/StarGaze.shtml.

During the academic year, physics and astronomy staff offer special astronomy-related activities at the local Harrisonburg Farmers

Market from 10 a.m. until noon. This event is weather-dependent and may include safe solar viewing, hands-on activities, and answering of space-related questions.

The John C. Wells planetarium also hosts other special events during the year, including science talks and movie screenings. Check the home page for current information and schedules.

Abbitt Planetarium and Observatory
Newport News, Virginia

Features: mobility access,
assistive listening access

Virginia Living Museum

Abbitt Planetarium and Observatory
Virginia Living Museum
524 J. Clyde Morris Boulevard
Newport News, Virginia 23601
www.thevlm.org

The Virginia Living Museum is home to the Abbitt Planetarium and Observatory. The museum is wheelchair accessible; three wheelchairs are available on a first-come, first-served basis for visitors to borrow during their stay at the museum.

The Abbitt Planetarium is wheelchair accessible and can accommodate three wheelchairs per show. The planetarium show schedule varies during the year, so it is best to check the current schedule through the museum website.

An assistive listening system with volume-adjustable headsets is available for all planetarium shows.

Although the Abbitt Planetarium does not have sign language interpreters, they are able to provide sufficient lighting for any interpreters that accompany hearing-impaired guests. The planetarium staff can also supply a written copy of the planetarium show script, by request.

The Abbitt Observatory is accessible via an elevator. Weather permitting, the Abbitt

Observatory offers daily safe viewing of the Sun and other sky objects. Several telescopes are available, including a 16-inch Meade telescope. This telescope is mounted on a unique pier that is height-adjustable, making it accessible to a person who is seated.

Ethyl IMAX Dome and Planetarium
Richmond, Virginia

Features: mobility access,
captioning (for selected IMAX films)

Science Museum of Virginia

Ethyl IMAX Dome and Planetarium
Science Museum of Virginia
2500 West Broad Street
Richmond, Virginia 23220
www.smv.org

The Science Museum of Virginia is wheelchair accessible, as are a majority of the exhibits. Two wheelchairs and one electric scooter are available on a first-come, first-served basis.

An exhibition called Science on a Sphere offers visitors a dynamic visual display of earth science and astronomy images projected on a large sphere model. The museum also features a life-sized space station slice in Out of This World and Virginia's Moon rock in Cosmic Visions.

The Ethyl IMAX Dome and Planetarium are the same theater at the Science Museum of Virginia. IMAX and planetarium shows are presented at different times in this five-story IMAX dome. Six wheelchairs can comfortably fit in each show.

Captioning is not available for planetarium shows but is available for many of the IMAX films. Captions are displayed onto Rear Window reflector screens that fit in the cup holders of seats. Theater staff provides the reflectors and will instruct anyone in this captioning system, including where to sit and how to use the device.

The Live Sky planetarium show is presented on the third Friday of the month. Weather permitting, members of the Richmond Astronomical Society will share views of the night sky through their portable telescopes in front of the Museum for Sky Watch after the planetarium show. Check the museum website for current times and dates of the planetarium show and observatory session.

WASHINGTON

Battle Point Astronomical Association
Battle Point, Washington

Features: mobility access (limited),
low vision access

Battle Point Astronomical Association

Battle Point Astronomical Association
Battle Point Park
Bainbridge Island, Washington 98110
www.bpastro.org

The Battle Point Astronomical Society presents observing sessions at the Edwin Ritchie Observatory and Planetarium shows at the John Rudolph Planetarium. Both facilities are located in one building within Battle Point Park. The building was part of a Navy radio transmission station that was used to communicate to submarines during World War II. It is built like a bunker.

Accessible parking is available with advance notice. A portable ramp allows visitors in wheelchairs entrance to the planetarium on the first floor.

The observatory is located on the building roof and is reached by climbing three flights of stairs. However, the telescopic image may be broadcast to a monitor at ground level with advance notice.

Willard Smith Planetarium
Seattle, Washington

Features: mobility access

Pacific Science Center

Willard Smith Planetarium

Pacific Science Center

200 2nd Avenue N

Seattle, Washington 98116

www.pacificsciencecenter.org

The Willard Smith Planetarium is located in Seattle's Pacific Science Center. The science center houses exhibits plus the planetarium, a laser dome, and two IMAX theaters.

The PACCAR IMAX Theater accommodates ten wheelchairs, and the Boeing IMAX Theater can accommodate six wheelchairs. Two wheelchairs can fit in the Willard Smith Planetarium.

All of the general exhibits are wheelchair accessible, and some components include multisensory experiences.

Wheelchairs are available on a first-come, first-served basis. Personal aides (assistants) accompanying a guest with a disability receive complimentary general admission to the Pacific Science Center. There is a limit of one aide per guest.

Copies of IMAX Theater show scripts are available in advance, by request.

The programs in the planetarium are presented live and conducted by a teacher who responds to questions, interests, and needs of the guests. These shows focus on the night sky, current space science, and astronomy. Three to eight planetarium shows are presented each day.

WEST VIRGINIA

National Radio Astronomy Observatory
Green Bank, West Virginia
Features: mobility access

NRAO Green Bank

National Radio Astronomy Observatory
Route 28 and 92
Green Bank, West Virginia 24944
www.nrao.edu/index.php/learn/gbsc

The National Radio Astronomy Observatory (NRAO) is a radio telescope facility. The Science Center is wheelchair accessible and offers a variety of facilities to explore, including exhibits, a gift shop, and a cafe. There is no admission charge to visit the Science Center.

The Green Bank Observatory is home to several radio telescopes including the 328-foot (100 m) Robert C. Byrd telescope, the world's largest fully steerable radio telescope.

The radio telescopes are very sensitive to interference, so cell phones may not be used.

Tours of the radio telescopes are available on wheelchair accessible buses. Tour tickets can be purchased in the Science Center building. Check the home page for current tour information and pricing.

WISCONSIN

Barlow Planetarium
Menasha, Wisconsin
Features: mobility access,
assistive listening access

Barlow Planetarium

Barlow Planetarium
University of Wisconsin–Fox Valley
1478 Midway Road
Menasha, Wisconsin 54952
www.barlowplanetarium.org

The Barlow Planetarium is located at the Fox Valley campus of the University of Wisconsin. Public Planetarium shows are presented Tuesdays through Saturdays in the afternoon.

The planetarium is wheelchair accessible; four wheelchairs can be accommodated for each show. An assistive listening system is available for planetarium shows.

During the winter months, the Barlow Planetarium presents evening laser shows with rock music. The images are bright abstract designs that often flash and pulse. The laser shows are projected on the dome using full color and full dome laser projection technology and ten thousand watts of digital sound. Check the Barlow Planetarium home page for current planetarium and laser show schedule.

Students in grades 3 through 8 may be interested in the summer space-related workshops and courses offered by the planetarium staff.

Manfred Olson Planetarium
Milwaukee, Wisconsin

Features: mobility access (planetarium only)

University of Wisconsin

Manfred Olson Planetarium

University of Wisconsin–Milwaukee

Physics–Planetarium Building

1900 East Kenwood Boulevard

Milwaukee, Wisconsin 53211

Planetarium.uwm.edu

The Manfred Olson Planetarium is located in the physics building on the University of Wisconsin–Milwaukee campus. The building is located in the corner of Kenwood Boulevard and Cramer Street.

To access the wheelchair accessible entrance, use the path between the physics building and the engineering and mathematics building, off Cramer Street. The entrance to the physics building is on the right. Once you are inside the building, the planetarium door is immediately to your left.

The planetarium is wheelchair accessible; up to six wheelchairs can comfortably fit inside.

Public planetarium shows are presented on most Friday evenings and on selected Wednesday afternoons.

Stargazing is offered at selected times during the year. The observatory is not wheelchair accessible. Check the website for current show and stargazing schedules.

BEYOND THE UNITED STATES—CANADA

Buckhorn Observatory
Ontario, Canada

Features: mobility access, low vision access

Buckhorn Observatory

Buckhorn Observatory
2254 County Road 507
Buckhorn, Ontario, Canada K0L 1J0
www.buckhornobservatory.com

Buckhorn Observatory is located about an hour and a half north of Toronto, Canada, in an area called the Kawarthas. Visitors view the night sky with telescopes and binoculars from April to October. Buckhorn Observatory is run by two amateur astronomers, John and Deb Crossen. Visitors pay a small fee to pay for equipment maintenance.

The large observatory building is wheelchair accessible, but the available restrooms are not. Accessible parking is near the observatory front doors.

The evening program begins with a naked-eye tour of the sky on a wheelchair-accessible deck with benches. Viewing then moves into the observatory building.

Images from the telescope can be relayed to a monitor for mobility and low vision access. Portable telescopes are also available with height-adjustable tripods.

For further accessibility questions, email johnstargazer@xplornet.com.

BEYOND THE UNITED STATES— ENGLAND

Thinktank Science Museum
Birmingham, England

Features: mobility access, low vision access, tactile materials, BSL (by request)

Thinktank Science Museum

Thinktank Science Museum
Millennium Point
Curzon Street
Birmingham, West Midlands B4 7XG
United Kingdom
www.thinktank.ac

The Thinktank Science Museum is located in Birmingham, England, and features interactive exhibits, a planetarium, and and a giant screen cinema. The museum is wheelchair accessible and also has wheelchairs available for loan.

Printed copies of planetarium show scripts, including copies in large print, are available for use before or during the presentation. Groups may request, in advance, a British Sign Language (BSL) interpreter for the planetarium show. A BSL video about the Thinktank Science Museum is available on the Thinktank home page.

Most of the exhibits have large print captions, and large print brochures are available upon request. A limited number of magnifying glasses are available for loan.

Astronomy books with Braille and tactile illustrations are available for use during museum hours. All of the live planetarium shows are designed to follow the tactile illustrations in the book **Touch the Stars**.

Accessible Resources and Vendors

Attention Deficit Hyperactivity Disorder (ADHD)

Helping Children with Attention Deficit Disorder
http://www.helpguide.org/mental/adhd_add_parenting_strategies.htm

Attention Deficit Hyperactivity Disorder (ADHD)

National Institute of Mental Health
http://www.nimh.nih.gov/health/publications/attention-deficit-hyperactivity-disorder/complete-index.shtml

Adobe

Adobe Photoshop Elements software
www.adobe.com

Asthma

Center for Disease Control and Prevention
http://www.cdc.gov/asthma/

Diabetes
American Diabetes Association
http://www.diabetes.org/

American Foundation for the Blind
Blindness statistics and resources
www.afb.org

American School for the Deaf
Education and resources for persons who are
deaf or heard of hearing
www.asd-1817.org

American Thermoform Corp.
Swell Form thermal expansion machine and
Swell Touch Paper
www.americanthermoform.com

Arthritis
Centers for Disease Control and Prevention
http://www.cdc.gov/arthritis/

AssistiveWare
Proloquo2Go AAC communication app for
iPhone, iPod, or iPad
http://itunes.apple.com/WebObjects/MZStore
.woa/wa/viewSoftware?id=308368164

Autism Families CONNECTicut

Coordinates social, recreational, and educational opportunities for children on the autism spectrum in Connecticut

www.autismfamiliesct.org

Autism Speaks

Resources, services and advocacy about autism spectrum disorder

www.autismspeaks.org

Autism spectrum disorder statistics

Centers for Disease Control and Prevention

http://www.cdc.gov/ncbddd/autism/data.html

Braille Institute

Blindness statistics and resources

http://brailleinstitute.org

Cancer

National Cancer Institute

http://www.cancer.gov/

Celestron Telescopes

FirstScope telescope

www.celestron.com

Chronic fatigue syndrome

Symptoms from the Mayo Clinic
http://www.mayoclinic.com/health/
chronic-fatigue-syndrome/DS00395/
DSECTION=symptoms

DFM Engineering

ARE-125 Articulated Eyepiece
www.dfmengineering.com

Dr. Temple Grandin's Official Autism Web Site

Temple Grandin's books and DVDs on autism
spectrum disorder
www.templegrandin.com

DynaVox Mayer-Johnson

ACC communication devices
www.dynavoxtech.com

Edmund Scientific

Astroscan telescope
www.scientificsonline.com

Epilepsy

Centers for Disease Control and Prevention
http://www.cdc.gov/Epilepsy/

Far Laboratories
Dyna Pier Angled Telescope Mount
http://www.dynapod.com/

Gallaudet University
Deaf population statistics
http://libguides.gallaudet.edu/print_content
.php?pid=119476&sid=1029158

Humanware
Picture in a Flash (PIAF) thermal expansion
machine
www.humanware.com

iDev2.com
iSign ASL application for iPhone, iPod Touch,
and iPad.
http://itunes.apple.com/app/isign/id288858200

Lyme Disease
Symptoms from the Mayo Clinic
http://www.mayoclinic.com/health/lyme-disease/
DS00116/DSECTION=symptoms

Microsoft
PowerPoint software
www.microsoft.com

National Braille Press
Touch the Stars (tactile book)
www.nbp.org/ic/nbp/TOUCH.html

National Federation of the Blind
The NFB improves blind people's lives through advocacy, education, research, technology, and programs encouraging independence and self-confidence.
www.nfb.org

National Center for Blind Youth in Science
Blind Science Online Portal
www.blindscience.org

Orion Telescopes
Dobsonian Telescopes
www.telescope.com

Sickle Cell Disease
Centers for Disease Control and Prevention
http://www.cdc.gov/ncbddd/sicklecell/index.html

Space Telescope Science Institute
Tactile Astronomy Picture of the Month
http://amazing-space.stsci.edu/tactile-astronomy

Traumatic Brain Injury

National Institute of Neurological Disorders and Stroke (NINDS)

http://www.ninds.nih.gov/disorders/tbi/tbi.htm

United Cerebral Palsy (UCP)

Educates, advocates and provides support services to ensure a life without limits for people with a spectrum of disabilities.

http://affnet.ucp.org/

United States Department of Labor Office of Disability Employment Policy (ODEP)

Provides national leadership by developing and influencing disability employment-related policies and practices affecting an increase in the employment of people with disabilities.

http://www.dol.gov/odep/

U.S. Department of Commerce

Status of People with Disabilities, 1997 Census Brief

www.census.gov/prod/3/97pubs/cenbr975.pdf

U.S. Department of Justice
Americans with Disabilities Act homepage
www.ada.gov

U.S. Department of Justice
Revised (2011) ADA regulations for service
animals
http://www.ada.gov/service_animals_2010.htm

You Can Do Astronomy LLC
Accessibility consulting for science museums,
planetariums, and observatories; speaker on
topics relating to astronomy and the need for
accessible science; presentation of accessible
space science workshops for teachers and
students; design of tactile materials
www.youcandoastronomy.com

Astronomy and Space Science Resources

Learn more about astronomy and space science from these resources.

American Astronomical Society
www.aas.org

Astronomy Education Review
Journal for astronomy educators
http://aer.aas.org/

Astronomy Magazine
www.astronomy.com

Astronomical Society of the Pacific
www.astrosociety.org

**National Aeronautics
and Space Administration**
www.nasa.gov

Sky & Telescope Magazine
www.skyandtelescope.com

Index

NOTES

NOTES

NOTES

NOTES

NOTES

NOTES

NOTES